MEASUREMENT IN DIRECT PRACTICE

SAGE HUMAN SERVICES GUIDES, VOLUME 59

SAGE HUMAN SERVICES GUIDES

A series of books edited by ARMAND LAUFFER and CHARLES D. GARVIN. Published in cooperation with the University of Michigan School of Social Work and other organizations.

A **SAGE** HUMAN SERVICES GUIDE **59**

MEASUREMENT IN DIRECT SOCIAL WORK PRACTICE

**Betty J. Blythe
and
Tony Tripodi**

*Published in cooperation with the University of
Michigan School of Social Work*

SAGE PUBLICATIONS
The International Professional Publishers
Newbury Park   London   New Delhi

To Robert Alfred Blythe and Andrew Robert Kitto

For information address:

SAGE Publications, Inc.
2455 Teller Road
Newbury Park, California 91320
E-mail: order@sagepub.com

SAGE Publications Ltd.
6 Bonhill Street
London EC2A 4PU
United Kingdom

SAGE Publications India Pvt. Ltd.
M-32 Market
Greater Kailash I
New Delhi 110 048 India

Printed in the United States of America

Library of Congress Cataloging-in-Publication Data

Blythe, Betty J.
    Measurement in direct practice / Betty J. Blythe and Tony Tripodi.
        p.   cm. — (Sage human services guides ; 59)
        Bibliography: p.
    ISBN 0-8039-3080-1
    1. Social service — Evaluation — Statistical methods.   I. Tripodi,
Tony.   II. Title.   III. Series: Sage human services guides ; v. 59.
    HV29.B58   1989
    361.3′2′068—dc20   89-10236
                                                                CIP

97   98   99   00   01   02   03   13   12   11   10   9   8   7

CONTENTS

FOREWORD

A fundamental issue in the evaluation of direct practice is that of measurement. If variables pertaining to practice effectiveness are not devised, it is impossible to determine whether maintenance, prevention, or change goals in direct practice are being achieved. We social workers are now committed to evaluating practice. We are increasingly subject to agency and client accountability, and the Council on Social Work Education's accrediting body has recently included guidelines requiring that master's degree programs in schools of social work offer content on evaluating practice, in research and practice courses, and in the field.

At a recent conference on Empiricism in Clinical Practice sponsored by the School of Social Work at the State University of New York at Albany, leading researchers in direct practice convened to discuss current and future issues to advance the integration of research in practice. Highlighted were themes indicating that the research paradigms most often taught were not readily applicable in practice settings because of their complexity and the enormous number of assumptions required for their use. Essentially, these researchers advocated more direct relevance of research tools to practice objectives and to the processes of practice. They also noted that it is first necessary that appropriate and relevant measurement be developed prior to implementing simple or complex single-case designs. Therefore, many participants stressed that empirically based practice endeavors could not be fully implemented until practitioners understand and apply principles of measurement in their practice.

This book emphasizes the conceptualization and use of measurement concepts and principles in relationship to decisions routinely made in direct practice. The authors apply measurement ideas to a phase model of practice that enables them to illustrate, with examples from a wide variety of practice perspectives, how to use measurement to assess problems, develop objectives, and monitor progress in attaining these objectives, and how to apply the information derived from measurement to practice decisions such as referral, termination, shifting treatment intensities and modalities. They illustrate how graphic analyses can monitor the achievement of specific objectives, and how measurement concepts can be employed for measuring change or lack of change, irrespective of the work of practice. In essence, Blythe and Tripodi demonstrate that a social worker does not need to be a behaviorist, neo-Freudian, cognitive therapist, family therapist, or a member of any other therapeutic school of thought to effectively utilize measurement theory for monitoring and evaluating practice. The strong feature of this book is that they illustrate this quite well, but at the same time constantly relate measurement to decisions that take place in the process of practice, a key ingredient that seems to have been ignored or emphasized very little in our training of social work students to evaluate their practice.

This book can also be used by practicing social workers, many of whom were trained during an era of practice-research dichotomies and resistances. Blythe and Tripodi emphasize the use of research as a tool to facilitate practice, and they provide a conceptualization that is easy to understand, relevant, and practical. This book provides important basic knowledge that can serve as a first step for those who wish to increase further their research skills for practice. Thus, although it is not a comprehensive research text, it can serve as a primer in using and integrating elementary research concepts for promoting direct practice.

— Scott Briar

PREFACE

This is a book that focuses on the integration of basic research concepts in a problem-solving model of direct clinical practice. We believe the key to integrating research in practice so that it is empirically based is in the way in which notions of measurement are defined and explicated. Accordingly, emphasis has been placed on how basic research concepts about measurement can play an important part in facilitating practice-related decisions. This book, therefore, is intended as a primer for social work practitioners, as a guide for incorporating elementary research principles in practice, and as a frame of reference for the further integration of research concepts and ideas.

B. J. B.
T. T.

Chapter 1

INTRODUCTION

The integration of practice and research to form empirically based practice has been the goal of many scholars and practitioners in the social work profession for three decades (Bloom & Fischer, 1982; Briar & Miller, 1971; Briar, 1973; Goldstein, 1962; Jayaratne & Levy, 1979; Maas, 1979; Tripodi, 1988; Tripodi & Epstein, 1980). As defined by Siegel (1984, p. 329), empirically based practice requires that a social worker:

"1. makes maximum use of research findings,

2. collects data systematically to monitor the intervention,

3. demonstrates empirically whether or not interventions are effective,

4. specifies problems, interventions, and outcomes in terms that are concrete, observable, and measurable,

5. uses research ways of thinking and research methods in defining clients' problems, formulating questions for practice, collecting assessment data, evaluating the effectiveness of interventions, and using evidence,

6. views research and practice as part of the same problem-solving process, and

7. views research as a tool to be used in practice."

Despite considerable efforts to promote this approach, practitioners have not widely adopted the principles of empirically based practice (Gingerich, 1984; Richey, Blythe, & Berlin, 1987). To some extent, these stipulations have been incorporated by social workers with behavioral orientations toward practice, as is evident in texts by Martin Bloom and Joel Fischer (1982) and Srinika Jayaratne and Rona Levy (1979). However, the majority of social workers are eclectic and have theoretical orientations that require less specificity and preplanning of interventions than do behavioral methods. In fact, during her tenure as the editor-in-chief of *Social Work*, Carol Meyer (1984) attributed the difficulty in integrating research and practice, in part, to the following:

1. "... preoccupation with effective practice and effectiveness defined in such a way that it could be counted ... "
2. "Most of the research methodology in use today requires the kind of narrow definition of problems and specification of variables that only behaviorist practice can provide concretely; thus it is all but impossible for practitioners who work in different modes to participate in research."
3. "A third issue is the current emphasis on change in clients as the phenomenon to be studied."

This book attempts to address the issues that have inhibited the integration of practice and research, as outlined by Meyer and others (Davis, 1985; Ivanoff, Blythe, & Briar, 1987; Heineman, 1981; Kagle, 1982; Ruckdeschel & Farris, 1981; Thomas; 1978).

PURPOSE OF THE BOOK

We believe that the above difficulties can be overcome and that the integration of research and practice is not only desirable but also possible for all modes of practice. Further, we are convinced that the key to integration lies in the conception of the measurement process. Existing technology is sufficient to allow research concepts and principles to be used as tools in all models of direct practice. Therefore, the purpose of this book is to provide a perspective on measurement that will enable social workers to use research methodology to facilitate their practice. In our perspective on the process of measurement, different types of measurement are presented, including classificatory or nominal data obtained by qualitative procedures to reflect such phenomena as clients' psychological states and environmental conditions. Various types of measurement are illustrated with examples from social work practice in a wide range of practice settings. Moreover, a phase model of direct practice is provided to illustrate the integration of research in specific tasks performed by social workers.

This book is intended for social workers who have little background and experience in social research methods. It is an introductory book that can be used as a supplementary text for courses in research or direct practice at either the senior level in undergraduate education or for beginning courses in graduate schools of social work. More importantly, it is believed that this book will be instructive for practitioners engaged in direct practice in social agencies. A major purpose is to introduce social workers to various ways in which research concepts can potentially help them in their practice.

The book is not intended to be exhaustive in its coverage of research concepts and in its references to practice situations. It is not a primer on single-subject design nor a text on program evaluation or advanced methods of clinical research. It does, however, explain basic research principles and provide a framework for applying those principles in direct practice.

A PHASE MODEL OF DIRECT PRACTICE

The focus of this book is on social workers in social agencies who work directly with clients. Direct practice is defined as the use of social work interventions with individuals, couples, families, and groups to enhance their intra- and interpersonal functioning. Potential generalized objectives of direct practice include encouraging changes in client systems (including individuals, couples, families, and groups), and/or changes in their environments; facilitating adaptation to significant others and the environment; and preventing social, psychological, and economic dysfunction.

The phase model of practice presented in this book incorporates a problem-solving approach. Although it is impossible to characterize completely the work of social workers into one conceptual system, a problem-solving model is useful in that it depicts social work tasks that occur in a wide range of practice settings. Such a model has also been used to show similarities between practice and research (Siegel, 1984; Tripodi, 1974; Tripodi & Epstein, 1980) and to illustrate different sequential phases of direct practice. In general, problem-solving models involve defining and specifying clients' problems, delineating and implementing strategies and/or interventions, and making systematic observations of the extent to which the strategies and interventions solve the problems.

The phases employed in our model of practice are assessment, planning interventions; implementing interventions; and termination and follow-up. Each of the phases contains specific tasks that social workers are engaged in when they work with client systems in direct practice. These phases have been used in a variety of educational and agency contexts to train social workers with diverse theoretical perspectives. Moreover, research methods can be incorporated in each of the phases. Our phase model is heuristic in that it specifies places in practice where certain key functions can be delineated. By necessity, it is also somewhat artificial, which is true of most didactic presentations that tend to clarify but also simplify the world of practice. The phases are presented as orderly and sequential, but there is overlap among the phases. Moreover, some types of practice require a long time for the phases to occur; whereas, other types involve short-term interventions in which phases may occur almost simultaneously. Residential treatment of emotionally disturbed adolescents is an example of the former, Traveler's Aid of the latter.

Assessment is the beginning phase of practice in which the social worker obtains a sense of the problems and issues confronting clients. In addition to determining the appropriate client system to serve and the client's eligibility for services from the social agency, the social worker also decides whether he or she can provide interventions for the client problem(s) and, if necessary, refers the client to other community agencies. If the worker intends to assist the client, the problems are inventoried and more fully specified. In doing so, the social worker attempts to answer such questions as:

- What are the most important problems, if any, for the client?
- Are the problems sufficiently serious so that intervention is justified?
- Do the problems involve prevention, maintenance, or change of behaviors, beliefs, cognitions, affective states, or familial and/or environmental conditions?
- If the problems require change, what is the desired level of change?

Planning interventions is the second phase of direct practice. While the general type of interventions offered are determined by the policies and procedures of the social agency where they are employed, social workers typically have a wide range of discretion regarding the nature and extent of interventions used with clients. Having selected problems for intervention, the social worker decides on the target of intervention and who is to be involved (individual clients, significant others, community members, and so forth) in the intervention. General objectives are delineated and specific short- as well as long-term goals are usually defined. Based on prior experience, supervision, and the practice and research literature pertaining to the clients' problems, interventions to accomplish those objectives are chosen. To the extent that is possible, the interventions are proceduralized by specifying the exact conditions under which they will be applied (Thomas, 1984). Hypotheses are made that relate the attainment of intervention objectives to the implementation of interventions.

The social worker also decides on criteria for the attainment of intervention objectives in this phase. A preadolescent client served by a delinquency diversion project, instances of truancy from school, taking money from a parent's wallet without permission, and damaging a neighbor boy's bicycle may be indicators of delinquency and/or of failure to prevent a potentially delinquent child from engaging in delinquency. As another example, consider a pregnant teenager who has decided to relinquish her baby for adoption. The social worker's short-term objective might be to help the teenager accept this decision, while the long-term objective might be helping her avoid subsequent un-wanted pregnancies. Attainment of objectives might be assessed by the adolescent's positive attitudes toward herself in reference to the disposition of the baby, her knowledge about birth control, her recognition of a wide range of options and choices in her life and, ultimately, her effective utilization of contraceptives.

Once criteria for attaining intervention objectives are specified, the social worker devises a plan for monitoring the extent to which those objectives are achieved. Observational strategies and forms might be designed to assist in collecting the monitoring information. In other instances, existing measurement tools may be selected.

Implementing interventions involves testing specific interventions with clients. Plans for intervention are followed, and the social worker determines the extent to which conditions are sufficient for implementation. The social worker must determine if the procedures specified in the last phase can be implemented and if the client can be involved in the intervention as specified. For example, if a parent is learning to replace harsh methods of discipline with child management techniques through role-play practice, is the client willing to follow procedures such as practicing statements that set clear limits with the worker playing the child's role and the parent playing herself? Further, is the parent willing to try the limit-setting statements outside of the session with her own children? Thus, the social worker decides whether the intervention plans can be followed and locates facilitators and barriers to implementation. In essence, the social worker attempts to make intervention operative and then monitors its feasibility.

The plan for monitoring client progress toward the objectives also is implemented in this phase, sometimes simultaneously with the implementation of the intervention and sometimes before the intervention is implemented. Based on the information yielded by the monitoring plan and other objectives, the social worker decides whether improvement is occurring and, if so, whether the rate of improvement is consistent with expectations or should be accelerated (by revising the intervention in some way). If no improvement takes place, the social worker may elect to modify the intervention, substitute a new intervention, or continue the intervention at the same pace (expecting improvement later in the process).

The social worker also may locate new problems that appear to take precedence over the one's identified initially, thereby causing a revision in the intervention plan. A medical social worker, for example, may specify the objective of having a husband assist his wife (the patient) in taking medication. The planned intervention of prompting and reinforcement by the husband might not be implemented because of negative interactions between spouses, which are observed by the worker when talking with the couple. As a result, an objective regarding the positive aspects of the couple's relationship might be targeted, with the intervention hypothesis that a positive relationship between spouses is more likely to result in cooperation between the couple and, ultimately, facilitate the patient's rate of compliance with medication.

Termination and follow-up is the final phase of practice. Termination of an intervention may occur when all of the objectives related to that intervention are realized, or when it is decided that the intervention cannot be implemented successfully, or when the intervention has been successfully implemented but no progress has been achieved on the objectives. In other instances, termination is not planned, as when the client prematurely elects to discontinue treatment. Or, the social worker may discontinue work with the client because of job transfer, sickness, or even death.

Termination can be restricted to one or more objectives, in which case the social worker continues to see the client but they work on a different set of objectives. Thus, an intervention to accomplish one objective may be terminated, while another intervention employed to achieve another objective is still in place or an intervention to reach a new objective is initiated. For example, a behavior modification intervention might be used to achieve weight loss, while a psychodynamically oriented intervention is employed to increase a client's understanding of his negative feelings toward his mother. If the client's understanding is increased but weight loss does not occur, the psychodynamic intervention might be terminated while the worker continues to see if the client achieves weight loss in response to the behaviorally oriented intervention.

After interventions are terminated, follow-up observations can occur to determine whether progress continues to be maintained with respect to the objectives. If progress is not maintained, the social worker decides whether or not to reinstitute the intervention and/or modify it or to substitute another intervention. Several types of follow-up are possible. First, there may be a planned follow-up at designated time periods, after all services to the client have been terminated, to observe the extent to which progress is maintained as well as to determine whether the client experiences any new problems. Second, follow-up might take place as the frequency of intervention sessions are diminished over time (for example, appointments are reduced from once a week to once every two weeks to once a month). Third, follow-up may occur when one objective has been attained with one intervention, while one or more interventions are still operative for one or more other objectives with that same client.

MEASUREMENT PERSPECTIVES

Measurement, broadly defined, is " . . . any endeavor attempting to assign numerals or symbols to (indicants of) properties of objects according to specified rules . . . " (Bostwick & Kyte, 1985, p. 151). The process of measurement includes specifying the type of data (qualitative or quantitative) necessary to operationally define a concept; categorizing data into one of four measurement scales (nominal or classificatory, ordinal, interval, or ratio); determining whether the resulting variable is a measurable dimension of a concept and is reliable and valid; and assessing the feasibility of using the variable for research and social work practice.

Quantitative data (such as a score on a college entrance exam) are already categorized into a measurement scale. In other words, numbers have been assigned to indicate different levels or categories of a variable. Qualitative data (such as responses to open-ended questions, narrative documents, and unstructured observations) can readily be transformed to measurement scales, particularly nominal scales, which require only that categories be mutually exclusive (nonoverlapping) and exhaustive (cover all possibilities). Since the simplest variables consist of two categories of a dimension or property of a concept, the following are illustrative: placement of children for adoption could be categorized into *placed* or *not placed;* a client's mood might be categorized as *anxious* or *not anxious,* and a patient's compliance with a medical regimen could be categorized as *compliant* or *noncompliant.* Ordinal measurement scales can also include qualitative data. In addition to classifying information into categories, ordinal scales must have order between adjacent categories. For example, a social worker might categorize and rank order clients within a group on dimensions such as positive relationships with other group members, willingness to share information, and degree of manifest depression. Thus, an ordinal scale to indicate the willingness to share information might have three points or categories: high level of willingness to share, medium level of willingness, and low level of willingness. Besides involving a rank ordering of categories, interval and ratio scales follow prescribed rules that allow one to count quantities of a dimension. Weight, height, number of counseling sessions attended, number of items correct on a knowledge test, number of facilitative comments made by each group member, number of temper tantrums per day, and frequency of sexual intercourse are examples. Interval and ratio scales are distinguished by one characteristic. Ratio scales have a conceivable absolute zero point, whereas interval scales do not; both types of scales have properties of classification, order, and equal distance between adjacent categories.

The process of measurement includes specifying rules for identifying variables. This is a systematic procedure whereby anyone following the rules should arrive at identical categorizations of quantitative or qualitative data into one of the four measurement scales. Suppose an adoption agency wants to keep records on the placement status of each child. A rule for the nominal-level variable regarding placement status would specify whether a boy living with his adoptive parents-to-be and waiting the completion of the adoption process would be considered *placed* or *not placed.* Adherence to the rules produces reliable (consistent) variables.

The arbitrary designation of numbers to categorize data into measurement scales does not necessarily signify that these scales represent the concepts being defined. The process of measurement also includes an estimation of the validity of the concept being measured. How representational and relevant is the variable? Is it accurate? For example, attendance at a family therapy session may imply satisfaction with the intervention. Particularly if those who attend regularly also rate themselves as "satisfied" with the intervention, there is some indication of validity. On the other hand, attendance would not necessarily be a valid measure of client satisfaction if all family members are coerced to attend regularly (as when a state child protective services agency requires family therapy if the children are to remain in their parents' care).

The purpose of measurement is to allow for systematic classification and comparison. It enables one to consider whether or not change occurs and, depending on the type of measurement scale employed, the degree of that change. As Carol Meyer (1984) implied, change in behavior or even any type of change may not be a particular objective with all clients. If they are conceptualized and operationalized in terms of measurement scales, however, the attainment of other kinds of objectives can be determined. Rather than changing behavior, objectives may relate to changing knowledge, attitudes, skills, or environments and situations. For example, one may seek to change abusive behavior of a son toward his elderly mother if they live together. Alternatively, there may be no objectives to change the behavior, but rather to change the location of the mother, that is, in a placement away from her son. Abusive behavior might be categorized into a ratio scale regarding the number of times the son abuses her, whereas placement could be categorized into a nominal scale of measurement.

If the social worker seeks to maintain the current situation of a client, exactly what is to be maintained must be specified, and then instances of nonmaintenance must be indicated. For example, a psychotic in remission may be out of the hospital and on a particular dosage of medication. Reversion to psychotic symptomatology and failure to take the required dosage of medication are indicators of a lack of maintenance. Hence, maintenance or nonchange can be observed by empirically demonstrating that change has not occurred. Correspondingly, a social worker might have an objective of prevention. Again, change conceptions can be employed to study the extent to which preventive objectives are realized. Suppose a social worker educates a group of teenagers about the properties and hazards of drugs in order to increase the teenagers' knowledge about drugs. Assuming that knowledge increases, it is further hypothesized that actual drug use will not occur. Accordingly, change would constitute the following: teenagers' knowledge about drugs should increase; prevention would be manifest if the teenagers' use of drugs does not increase after the social worker's efforts. Imagine that the social worker provides education without using measurement. The type of education provided may not lead to an increase in knowledge or may lead to an increase in knowledge but also in drug usage. Not only would the objectives not be achieved, but the clients may be harmed and the social worker would not know it. Moreover, the social worker may continue to offer the same education, potentially harming other clients.

Measurement is not related to any specific form of practice. First of all, objectives for clients can be identical although the models of practice and the interventions employed by social workers may differ. Immediate objectives for a delinquent teenager may include his spending more time at school and improving his grades; ultimately, it is hoped that the teenager will not be involved in any delinquent activities. These objectives can be measured. Interventions might be behavior modification, reality oriented therapy, guided group interaction, paradoxical therapy, family therapy, or psychodynamically oriented social casework. Second, different practice modalities can be specified in varying degrees. To the extent that the intervention follows precise procedures that can be formulated prior to interactions with clients, that intervention might be regarded as more amenable to measurement than other interventions that cannot be specified in advance. Many forms of social work practice depend upon the interactions that social workers have with clients, and although some of the parameters of intervention can be specified a priori, the bulk of the interventions cannot be so specified until interaction takes place. However, guidelines can be followed that give some prescriptive advice but which vary depending on the content of the interactions. Of course, after the interactions have taken place, they can more easily be measured by such things as type of activities employed: supportive statements, queries, interpretive remarks, and so forth.

Hudson (1985, pp. 187-189 indicates four axioms that are supposed to indicate the

" . . . powerful relationship . . . between measurement and social work practice. . . .

If you cannot measure a client's problem, it does not exist . . .

If you cannot measure a client's problem, you cannot treat it . . .

If you cannot measure an intervention, it does not exist . . .

If you cannot measure an intervention, you cannot administer it."

These statements can be misunderstood by social workers, depending upon their conception of measurement, as well as their philosophical orientation. Hudson's definition is consistent with logical positivism, but most certainly not with other philosophical orientations. The notion of existence regarding client's problems and interventions ultimately appears to be subjective and phenomenological. Our contention is that such statements imply that measurement of social work phenomena is more powerful than it is. Given the shortcomings of measurement and imperfect reliability and validity, it is, perhaps, more accurate to say that measurement can facilitate practice. There is no doubt in our minds that social work interventions, however nonspecified they are, will take place, although certain types of interventions may be more recognizable a posteriori than others. We believe social workers react negatively to statements such as these because they do not realize that much of measurement in social work involves the use of nominal or classificatory scales, rather than interval or ratio scales. In short, a client's problem can be measured if it can be distinguished from nonproblems.

Interventions consist of one or more variables. They can be proceduralized (that is, defined in a precise set of procedures) with some degree of specificity, as we shall show in subsequent chapters; however, whether interventions can be perfectly translatable into one or more variables is debatable. We believe that proceduralization is desirable and that it increases the possibility of replicating the intervention with the same client or with other clients. In facilitating replication, measurement becomes important beyond the treatment of a specific client. In dealing with one client system, measurement helps to reveal if change occurs or is not manifest (depending on the objective[s] for the client), as well as to indicate the degree of change when that is the expectation of the worker and client.

INCORPORATING MEASUREMENT IN DIRECT PRACTICE

We believe that incorporating measurement concepts and principles into direct practice is not only possible but necessary. Practice is facilitated by gathering and processing systematic information. Measurement can assist in reducing, as well as specifying, errors in assessment. It can be employed for developing hypotheses in the context of intervention. Measurement is instrumental for monitoring progress in the implementation of interventions and in the achievement of the client's and the social worker's objectives. Moreover, measurement can provide information related to decisions about termination with clients. In essence, measurement is a basic process that can contribute to gathering and analyzing information pertaining to each phase of practice.

This idea is not new. It was addressed by Harris Goldstein (1963) in his text on research methods when he attempted to show how practice can be more scientific by using the key concepts of operationalization, reliability, and validity. More recently, Thomas (1977) wrote a key paper on his BESDAS model, which includes the rudiments of empirically based practice so that practice could be more accountable, effective, and self-correcting. Thomas thought the components of practice should include specifying behavioral targets, selecting interventions based on empirically based knowledge, evaluating outcomes to be accountable, using feedback information to correct inefficient and ineffective practice, and employing data to guide practice. Tripodi and Epstein (1978) suggested that research concepts and principles could be integrated into problem-solving models of practice; and Jayaratne and Levy (1979) and Siegel (1984) defined the concept of empirically based practice in recent years. However, none of these approaches have illustrated how the basic process of measurement can be incorporated within the phases of direct practice, which is the fundamental aim of this book. Feedback from measurement, which includes the systematic gathering and processing of data, can be used to inform practitioners about decisions they must make and tasks they must accomplish to be of maximum assistance in helping clients.

The issue of practice effectiveness continues to be important for social work, and definitions of practice and of practice effectiveness spur controversies and acrimonious decisions among social workers (see the opinions of Ezell & McNeece, 1986 and of Rubin, 1986 and the summary by Ivanoff, Blythe, & Briar, 1987). However, there is substantial agreement that information can be used to inform practitioners. The debates are about definitions, practice objectives, and realistic expectations. In the spirit of empirically based practice, we believe that measurement concepts and principles can be used as tools by practitioners to gather data that address questions related to effectiveness and accountability. Therefore, in subsequent chapters we strive to illustrate how measurement concepts can be applied toward this end.

FORMAT OF THE BOOK

Chapter 2 is devoted to an explication of measurement, followed by four chapters organized around each sequential phase of practice. Tools for assessing client problems are introduced in Chapter 3. In addition, methods of interpreting information yielded by assessment procedures, including graphing and comparisons with normative data, are presented.

Chapter 4 illustrates the use of measurement procedures to aid in specifying intervention objectives, selecting interventions, and proceduralizing interventions. The identification and formulation of intervention hypotheses is also discussed.

Chapter 5 focuses on measurement procedures that facilitate the intervention phases. It details the use of measurement to ensure that interventions are implemented as intended. Various strategies for evaluating information collected with measurement devices are examined. Chapter 6 is concerned with termination and follow-up of interventions. The use of measurement to examine whether clients are maintaining, deteriorating, or improving in terms of the intervention objectives is presented. Decision making based on follow-up information is discussed. Chapters 2 through 6 include exercises that are aimed at helping the reader understand and apply the concepts and principles presented.

Chapter 2

MEASUREMENT

WHAT IS MEASUREMENT?

Measurement is a process that results in the consistent assignment of properties of people or objects so they can be classified, ordered, or counted. It enables one to identify and compare observations that pertain to the description and relationship of phenomena that are vital for social work. These observations might include developmental delays in a child, memory loss in an elderly person, or marital discord in a couple, as examples. The measurement process involves: (1) identifying a concept to be measured; (2) specifying an indicator of the concept; (3) operationally defining the data that are necessary for measurement and a way of ordering the information so it can be categorized into a variable; and (4) determining the reliability and validity of the variable.

A concept is a verbal or symbolic representation of some phenomenon in which one is interested. It may refer to characteristics of social workers or of their clients or client groups, to worker-client interactions, or to ecological and environmental phenomena. Concepts are the building blocks of any language and are necessary for professional discourse and record keeping in social work. Depression, ego strength, catharsis, transference, reinforcement, anxiety, coping, stress, change, adoption, chronic illness, tantrum, interpersonal relationship, group membership, income, intelligence, and reading ability are just a few of the phenomena that social workers may need to identify in their work with clients. As is evident, some concepts are very abstract, containing many ideas within them (such as coping), and some are much more concrete (such as a child's tantrum).

Before discussing the technical details of measurement, we shall illustrate the measurement process with the following example. Suppose a social worker is interested in measuring the concept of depression for a male client. If the concept is not specified further, it would be difficult for the worker to obtain any notion of the extent of depression, whether it changes over time, and whether an intervention should be used to change or maintain the client's level of depression. To obtain indicators of the concept, the worker might refer to the literature, the worker's previous experience with depressed clients, or to the experiences of other practitioners or researchers working with clients who sought help for depression. The worker would usually ask the current client to describe what depression means to him. Possible indicators might be crying, feelings of despair, loss of appetite, poor self-care, and loss of interest in work and recreational activities. When an operational definition is given, the indicator(s) must be specified as well as the tool for obtaining information to measure the concept of depression. An operational definition of depression might include the extent to which a person reports that he has symptoms indicative of depression: loss of appetite, crying, and so forth. A list of these symptoms could be provided to the client. The greater the number of symptoms checked by the client, the greater would be the extent of depression. Hence, a checklist of symptoms would be a possible tool for assessing the extent of depression. The information is categorized into a variable of depression, which would range from 0 symptoms to the total number of symptoms included on the checklist. This is one operational definition of depression, but there can be many other definitions. Operational definitions are arbitrary; they are neither right nor wrong, but they facilitate communication, replication, comparison, and the possibility of accumulating knowledge.

The utility of operational definitions of concepts is realized as reliability and validity are achieved. Imprecise definitions that cannot be used consistently (low reliability) and/or that bear no relevance to the concept being measured (low validity) are obviously useless and misleading. For the operational definition of depression above, there would be some evidence of reliability if the client would indicate consistently the number of symptoms that correspond to his mood. Evidence of validity would be present, if, for example, significant others observed the client having the same symptoms that he indicated on the checklist of symptoms. Thus, estimates of reliability and validity of the variable serve to indicate whether or not there is a shared understanding of the variable, and whether that variable has meaning.

PURPOSE OF THE CHAPTER

The purpose of this chapter is to provide some basic concepts of measurement that are essential for the subsequent chapters in which we show how measurement can be employed in each phase of direct practice. In this chapter, levels of measurement, types of variables in direct practice, characteristics of measurement, and types of measurement tools are discussed. The concepts contained herein are basic. If desired, further detail about these concepts is available elsewhere (Bloom & Fischer, 1982; Grinnell, 1985; Tripodi, 1983).

LEVELS OF MEASUREMENT: VARIABLES

A variable is a measurable dimension of a concept (such as depression) that contains two or more values. It is an indicator of a concept that is translated by means of an operational definition into one of four basic levels of measurement: nominal, ordinal, interval, or ratio scales. These four measurement scales form a continuum based on different types of information. Table 2.1 summarizes the properties and provides other examples of each level of measurement.

The simplest level of measurement is that of classification, the nominal scale. It contains two or more categories that are mutually exclusive and exhaustive. For example, a client may be regarded as coping or not coping with the death of her husband. Mutual exclusivity refers to the idea that the client can be assigned only to one category (*having* or *not having* symptoms), but not both. Mutual exhaustiveness refers to inclusiveness of the possible range of responses.

Ordinal measurement scales contain the properties of nominal scales plus the property of order between adjacent categories. A social worker in an adoption agency might have a great deal of information about six married couples' potential as adoptive parents, including years of marriage, age, income, employment history, religion, leisure activities, experiences with children, marital satisfaction, and physical health. Using that information, the worker might rank order the potential of the couples to be good adoptive parents from 1 (least potential) to 6 (most potential). As another example, a social worker might indicate the extent to which a client is anxious by using a rating scale that ranges

TABLE 2.1 Level of Measurement

Level of Measurement	Properties	Examples
Nominal	Classification into categories.	Male; female. Sexually abused; not sexually abused. Received vocational training; did not receive vocational training.
Ordinal	Classification into categories. Order between categories.	Under 3 years; 3 years or more. Lower class; middle class; upper class. Not at all defensive; somewhat defensive; extremely defensive.
Interval	Classification into categories. Order between categories. Equidistance between categories.	Calendar year. Temperature on Fahrenheit Scale.
Ratio	Classification into categories. Order between categories. Equidistance between categories. Absolute zero point.	Number of arguments. Number of previous hospitalizations. Number of supportive contacts with friends.

from 1 = *not at all anxious* to 5 = *anxious all of the time*. The categories 1 through 5 are mutually exclusive and exhaustive, and adjacent numbers bear a relationship of order. However, the arbitrary assignment of numerals does not designate equal distances between categories. In other words, the difference between 1 and 2 is not necessarily the same as the distance between 4 and 5. Thus, other symbols (such as *a* to *e*) can just as accurately be used to portray order, and variables can be used to refer to what many social workers would regard as qualitative information. Basically, the information only needs to be classified into categories, and then the categories must be ordered.

Interval measurement scales include properties of ordinal scales plus that of distance, that is, equal distances between adjacent categories. In assessing an elderly client's degree of social isolation, a social worker may be interested in the number of social contacts the client has had in a 2-week period. The number of social contacts in that period is an interval-level variable. Assuming the consistent application of the same definition for "social contact" (for example, telephone calls or in-person visits with a family member or friend lasting at least 5 minutes and having as a primary purpose a friendly exchange of news rather than of business), the difference between 9 and 10 social contacts is identical to the difference between 4 and 5 social contacts.

Ratio measurement scales contain the properties of interval scales plus that of natural origin, that is, a conception of a fixed, absolute, nonarbitrary 0 point that has meaning. Calendars have arbitrary origins, not natural ones. Hence, the variable of social contacts within a fixed time interval, as described above, does not have a natural origin. The variables of weight and income have natural origins.

Values from interval scales or ratio scales can be combined (added) and averaged, whereas values from nominal and ordinal scales cannot, since they do not reflect true properties of numbers. Although the procedures for specifying variables with nominal and ordinal levels are rigorous and systematic, those variables are less quantitative, by definition, than those obtained by interval or ratio scales. Since much more information is necessary to achieve interval and ratio than nominal and ordinal levels of measurement, it is not surprising to note that most of the variables we employ in social work and related social sciences are nominal and ordinal.

TYPES OF VARIABLES IN DIRECT PRACTICE

A list of all the possible kinds of variables encountered in social work practice would be endless since client characteristics and client problems are so varied. Nevertheless, a good deal of possible practice variables about clients can be illustrated by referring to the four types discussed below and outlined in Table 2.2. These types, for the most part, include variables that could change over time.

Type 1 designates client characteristics that can be observed by significant others, social workers, and the clients themselves. These variables include current and past physical and mental health statuses, such as the client's medical history, social information such as area and place of residence, income, education, marital status, and psychological or psychiatric classifications. Client characteristics that can show change are typically at the nominal scale of measurement. They show categorization into different groupings or by presence or absence of symptoms or traits. For example, a child lives with a family that neglects his needs. He could change from living with that family to living in another situation in which his needs are not neglected. An adult woman may change from being unemployed to being employed. A child may change from having symptoms of school phobia to having none.

TABLE 2.2 Typology of Practice Variables

Type 1	Client characteristics
Type 2	Moods, feelings, attitudes, beliefs, and values
Type 3	Knowledge, ability, and achievement
Type 4	Observable behavior

There also are client characteristics that are relatively fixed: gender, physical handicaps, ethnicity, nationality, and family events such as deaths, divorces, and marriages. Although fixed client characteristics, such as physical handicaps and chronic illness, do not change, social workers may still work with those clients with the goal of changing clients' perceptions of their status, as reflected in Type 2 variables, which refer to clients' moods, feelings, attitudes, beliefs, and values. These areas in which many variables could be devised are not observable by others; they are private perceptions that are reported by clients. Variables such as *felt comfort,* trust, and belief in one's own abilities as a parent can change for individual clients. These variables typically are reported on ordinal scales of measurement that reflect intensity or magnitude. They may be obtained from client responses to single-item scales or to combinations of items that are presented in the form of scales in a standardized instrument or other measurement tool. For example, a mother's attitude toward her daughter may be reflected on a scale indicating the degree of positive or negative attitudes ranging from very negative (−3) to neutral (0) to very positive (+3).

Type 3 includes knowledge, ability, and achievement, most often acquired in an academic setting. It is comprised of variables typically derived from paper-and-pencil tests. These variables reflect the number of items correctly answered on interval scales of measurement. For example, a variable reflecting arithmetic achievement may range from 0 to 50, the number of items on a test of arithmetic understanding. These variables may reflect change in response to interventions that include educational objectives.

Type 4 refers to observable behavior of clients. These variables are typically at interval or ratio levels of measurement, and they reflect frequencies (counts) of the behavior in question, and/or they might represent the duration or length of time for which a behavior occurs. For example, one variable might indicate the number of family quarrels in a designated time period; while another variable might refer to the percentage of time that was exclusively devoted to arguments.

The variables above are illustrative of types of variables that can occur during any phase of interpersonal practice: assessment, planning interventions, implementing interventions, and termination and follow-up. Social workers might be interested in some variables throughout all of the practice phases to gauge a client's progress. Or they may be interested in variables that are more strictly focused on a particular phase. For example, the social worker might be interested in measuring client satisfaction to provide some information about her or his implementation of a particular intervention. Variables within practice phases will be discussed in detail in subsequent chapters.

RELIABILITY

Reliability refers to the extent to which there is consistency in response on repeated applications of the measurement tool. There are different kinds of reliability that depend on the manner in which data are gathered to form variables. Type 1 (client characteristics) and type 4 (client behaviors) data can be obtained through observations made by social workers and significant persons other than the client, and one type of reliability to reflect consistency of observations is that of *interobserver agreement.* Interobserver agreement refers to the extent to which two or more independent observers of the same phenomenon agree in their observations on a provided response system. A social worker might have tape recorded an interview with a family, in which each family member has difficulty speaking to the other without making negative comments. Variables may have been devised to reflect the number of negative comments and the number of positive comments. For a segment of the interaction, the worker and his or her supervisor may independently listen to the tape and classify 50 sentences as either positive, neutral, or negative. If they agree on all 50 sentences, there is a high degree of interobserver reliability; correspondingly, a low degree of reliability would be evident if there is agreement for only 10 of the 50 sentences. An index to represent this kind of reliability is *percentage agreement,* the number of agreements divided by the total possible number of agreements times 100. The higher the percentage agreement, the higher the interobserver reliability, with 70 to 80% representing an adequate amount of reliability. In the above example, 10/50 x 100 = 20%, which is a low level of reliability.

Another form of reliability is that of *test-retest reliability.* It is the extent to which there is correspondence in the response of clients to a paper-and-pencil test, questionnaire, or inventory at two different points in time, or the extent to which there is agreement among independent observers over time. This type of reliability depends on the particular instrument or tool that is used. For example, a tool might be composed of 10 items that reflect symptoms of anxiety. A scoring system is devised such that higher numbers reflect high anxiety. A group of clients is administered the instrument. The next day the same clients are delivered the same items. To the extent that the scores are corresponding, the instrument is stable, that is, reliable over a brief period of time. It is assumed, however, that the clients' moods on the two different days are constant rather than variable, and that the clients are responding honestly.

Test-retest reliability would be especially appropriate for Type 3 data reflecting tests of knowledge, ability, and achievement and for appraising the consistency of behavioral observations at two or more points in time, that is Type 4 data. A correlation coefficient is an index that shows the degree of reliability over time. A correlation of 0 reflects no correspondence over time, while a correlation of 1 reflects complete consistency in response. Correlations of .8 and .9 reflect relatively high degrees of reliability. If one is interested in assessing change on a client variable, it is, of course, important to have an instrument that has high test-retest reliability.

Another type of reliability, *split-half reliability,* is useful when a tool is employed to obtain information for one variable and it contains many items. For example, Hudson has devised an instrument to assess a client's degree of marital satisfaction (Hudson, 1982). The instrument is comprised of 25 items, to which clients respond on a 5-point scale to each item which is intended to reflect marital satisfaction/dissatisfaction. To assess split-half reliability, responses to the odd-numbered items can be correlated with responses to the even-numbered items. A high correlation, assessed by a correlation coefficient, would indicate consistency of responses to different items, all reflecting the same variable of marital satisfaction/dissatisfaction. This type of reliability can be applied to Type 2 and Type 3 data.

A related type of reliability is that of *coefficient alpha,* which also reflects the internal consistency of responses to items in an instrument. Responses of ½ the items randomly selected from the instrument are correlated with responses to the remaining items. It is another index of inter-item consistency and is regarded as less subject to error than split-half reliability since there is no bias in the selection of items to correlate.

High reliability can be attained for variables related to social work practice by following some simple steps. First of all, the worker should consistently employ the same definitions and procedures of measurement. For example, a client might be asked to report his degree of anger on a rating scale ranging from *no anger* to *a constant state of anger*. To ascertain any changes in anger, repeated measures would be obtained.

If this is done, the client should have the same set of instructions and the same type of rating scale as was used previously, taking care to ensure that the report of anger is at the same time of day (for example, in the morning, ½ hour after waking). Second, the worker and the client should practice using the instrument and discuss its application. Third, the worker should ensure that the same kind of information is consistently available and used in forming the ratings. For example, the client should refer to the same kinds of information for rating anger, that is, shouting episodes, tenseness in the shoulders and neck, and so forth. If the client repeatedly completes the rating scale over a period of several weeks, the worker should occasionally verify that the client is using the same information to make the rating and that the definition of anger has not shifted. Fourth, the worker should establish sufficient rapport with the client so that there is confidence that the client trusts that the information will be used to help him or her. Fifth, the worker should convey to the client the importance of the information gathered, and show him or her, to the extent it is possible, how it will be used.

VALIDITY

It is not too difficult to establish high reliability for variables. However, consistency in responses does not necessarily mean the responses are correct. Two social workers may agree, for example, that a particular client is denying her young daughter's terminal illness, but their judgments may be in error. Residential treatment staff may agree about placing a child at a particular home for foster care, but their judgment may be wrong in the sense that the child's social adjustment may actually have deteriorated to such an extent that he is not ready to leave residential treatment. Or, to further illustrate, a client may consistently report that he is nonalcoholic, but he might be lying or his definition of alcoholism might differ from that of the worker. This sense of correctness and relevancy is what is vital in the concept of validity.

Technically, validity is the degree of correspondence between the concept being measured and the variable used to represent the concept. It is measuring what one thinks one is measuring. Validity implies accuracy in response as well as relevance of response. The more concrete the concept, the easier it is to obtain validity because the correspondence being sought between the concept and the variable is clear. For example, asking a client's age can be easily verified by comparing the client's statement with a document such as a birth certificate. On the other hand, a concept such as self-esteem is much more abstract and is more difficult to verify. This is because definitions of self-esteem differ, expectations of low and high self-esteem differ, and items that are supposed to reflect self-esteem are not consistently agreed upon by theoreticians.

Validity of a variable has two different aspects: *content* validity and *empirical* validity. *Content* validity refers to the validity of the content of the tool used to measure the concept. The contents of the measurement tool should relate logically to the concept, that is, they should be relevant, and they should be representative of all possible items that are indicative of the concept. For example, an inventory of relationship difficulties might contain a number of items indicative of interpersonal relationships with peers, authority figures, and others, and a client may be asked to indicate the extent to which she or he has difficulties on a scale ranging from *no difficulties* to *extreme tension and hostility* for a number of people. The contents are relevant to the degree that they represent difficulties (which would be defined further) as seen by clients and workers. The contents are representative to the extent that they provide a good sample of possible relationship difficulties. The exclusion of friends and family members from such an inventory would decrease validity, as compared to an inventory which included them, if the purpose were to measure the concept of relationship difficulty.

A more concrete concept might be that of a relationship difficulty with a particular person at a particular place during a specified event. For example, a mother may have difficulty relating to her teenage son at home during breakfast. One question about the relationship might be asked and one variable might reflect the degree of difficulty for that particular event. The relevance of that content would be determined by the social worker and the client. Whether or not the one item is representative, that is, sufficient to represent relationship difficulties between mother and son, could also be ascertained by discussion.

Gathering the information that is necessary to determine if a particular inventory or question is relevant to and representative of the client's problem is not simply a useless research exercise. In fact, a thorough assessment of the client problem often yields much of the necessary information. Moreover, the process of having an inventory against which to compare the client's specific problem, or of devising some questions or rating scales to assess the client's problem can provide the structure for a more in-depth and complete analysis of the components of the client's problem than often occurs in routine social work practice. Such additional information may help the client and worker better understand the problem and more readily identify increments of improvement or problem resolution. The detailed analysis also might suggest points of intervention to the worker that would have been overlooked in a less complete assessment.

The content validity of even less abstract variables is more easily specified. For example, if one is recording the number of times a child is absent from a class at school during a given week, the representativeness and relevance of the variable to the concept may be obvious in a question to the child's teacher, "How many times was the child absent from your class this week?" This question is the basic content of the instrument, and the variable of absence ranges, on a typical week of school from 0 to 5.

Empirical validity is another aspect of validity. It documents the empirical verification of predictions that are logical if the variable provides a measure of the concept. The more abstract the concept, the more predictions can be made about variables; to the extent that the predictions are verified, there exists empirical validity. Predictions are made about relationships of the variable to external criteria. Predictions can be made on the basis of current expectations, future expectations, and on complex theoretical speculations. Hence, empirical validity can be further divided into *concurrent* validity, *predictive* validity, and *construct* validity.

Predictions of a current relationship of an external criterion variable to a variable is *concurrent* validity. If a client responds "yes" to a question that asks whether or not he is a drug user, one would expect that the client's behavior would exhibit actual use of drugs, and that drugs would be present in his urine. Hence, significant others in a position to observe the client, assuming they feel secure enough to provide an honest report and are willing to do so, should report drug use. In addition, a urine analysis by a laboratory technician should reveal drug traces in the urine. These two different ways of measuring the same concept serve to verify the use of the procedure of simply asking the client. An index of concurrent validity is the degree of correlation between the results of the instrument on the variable being measured and an external criterion. In the drug use example, the question posed to the client would have high validity if the report of significant others and a urine analysis agree with the client's report.

Predictive validity is verification of a predicted relationship between the variable and an external criterion in the future. If a person indicates he is a child abuser in answer to a question about child abuse, one might expect, assuming he is not lying, that that person is more likely to be abusive to children at a future date than is one who says he is not currently a child abuser. Predictive validity is also ascertained by correlation coefficients.

A more complex type of validity is *construct* validity. It is employed when an abstract concept is embedded in some theory that describes the interrelationship of concepts. Predictions are made on the basis of a theoretically expected relationship between the variable being measured and another variable. A variable measuring the concept of anxiety may be correlated with other variables that are theoretically related. For example, one's theory of anxiety may lead to a hypothesis positing an inverse relationship between anxiety and learning. In other words, the more anxious a person is, the less likely he is to learn new material. Hence, verification of that hypothesis could add to the validity of the variable measuring the concept of anxiety. There may be a large number of theoretical expectations, however, and it may be impossible to verify all of them for a particular variable.

How much information is needed to decide whether a variable represents valid measurement? Under the following conditions, not a great deal of information is required: the concept is not embedded in theory and is relatively concrete; the instrument to measure the concept is not complex with many items; the purpose of the measurement is to be specific to a unique client rather than to all clients. Conversely, the attainment of validity is a complicated, incomplete process for the measurement of theoretical concepts.

With regard to the validity of variables in social work practice, at a minimum there should be agreement on the content validity of the variable, possible verification through concurrent validity, and an attempt to minimize errors when an instrument is employed to gather information from clients for categorization into the variable being measured.

MEASUREMENT ERRORS

Measurement errors diminish the reliability and validity of variables. They are discussed briefly here to increase the reader's sensitivity to other factors that could reduce the value of information obtained in assessing and monitoring client problems and progress toward intervention objectives. Errors that can occur during the process of measurement are: biases in the format of the instrument, biases in the instructions for using the instrument, biased predispositions of the respondent, and biases in the measuring environment. Instrument biases refer to the contents of instruments constructed for gathering data. There might be biases in the wording that predispose respondents to answer questions in fixed ways. For example, there may be leading questions in questionnaires which, if answered, force respondents to admit to problems or symptoms they do not have. The contents may be biased for or against special groupings: gender, racial minority, sexual minority, social class, and so forth. The items in a rating scale may be worded so that it is apparently desirable for the respondent to answer in one way rather than another, that is, there may be an element of social desirability apparent in the items, particularly if it is clear that respondents can be perceived favorably or unfavorably as a function of their answers. Note that even individual verbal or written questions posed to a client may be subject to instrument bias.

These possible sources of error are lessened when instruments are carefully constructed so that there is impartiality in their contents and so that it is clear that there are no socially desirable or set answers demanded or preferred by the social worker.

Instructional biases refer to biases in the instructions for using an instrument to gather data. An instructional set may be created when respondents believe they are to use the instrument in certain ways. Examples of possible instructional biases are observing more pathological behavior than is normally present when using observational forms, answering "yes" to questions that are favorable about an agency's policies, or acting as if there is improvement in interpersonal relationships as a result of believing that it would please the social worker.

Instructional biases are lessened when there is clarity and neutrality in the instructions. The tone of instructions should indicate the importance of the information, and the necessity for respondents to be as accurate as possible. Confidentiality of information and a specification of how and when it should be used is essential, and helps to increase the validity of the data gathering process. Clients may not be as honest in their responses as they could be if they perceive that the information gathered will be used against them rather than to help them. Respondents may be biased in the way in which they impose their own predispositions on instrument formats. There may be predispositions to respond positively, or "yes," to items, irrespective of their contents. Or, there may be tendencies in using rating scales such as these: avoiding the use of extreme positions, e.g., avoiding the use of responses such as "very satisfied" or "very dissatisfied" on questions related to treatment satisfaction; using the middle portion of scales, regardless of their contents; and generalizing a response from one scale to other scales, the *halo effect.* Moreover, respondents may show reactivity, that is, react to the instrument in such a way that there may be changes in their behavior or attitudes. For example, the process of weighing oneself may lead a respondent who had not been doing so to lose weight.

Respondent errors cannot be completely eliminated, but they can be minimized. Instruments that contain scales and questions can contain a balance of positively and negatively stated items and response alternatives. Middle portions of scales can be eliminated and/or the number of steps in a rating scale can be increased. Reactivity can be explored in order to understand whether or not it occurs with a particular instrument and for particular types of clients. This is simply done by using repeated observations of the measuring device to determine whether or not there is test-retest reliability, which implies lack of reactivity.

The measuring environment pertains to the interactions between respondents and social workers when data are gathered, as well as the environment where such data gathering occurs. Social workers might be inconsistent in their use of measuring devices, in their instructions, and in their attempts to clarify the instrument for respondents. Or, there may be environmental conditions, such as extreme temperatures or noise, that could reduce the instrument's reliability and validity. Training in the use of instruments is essential with an emphasis on consistency in application across clients as well as over time with the same clients. Environmental conditions should be pleasant, relaxed, and not conducive to fatigue, which in and of itself can lead to response errors.

THE RELATIONSHIP BETWEEN RELIABILITY AND VALIDITY

Since there are different kinds of reliability (interobserver agreement, test-retest, split-half reliability, and coefficient alpha) and validity (content, concurrent, predictive, and construct), their relationship varies with respect to the specific types of reliability and validity being considered. Different types of reliability also have different relationships, and it is possible for there to be high reliability in terms of internal consistency or interobserver agreement at one point in time, but with low reliability over two points in time. This is evident in a study of an intervention to enhance social competence in adolescents conducted by LeCroy and Rose (1986). A behavioral role-play test measured social skills of the adolescents and yielded information on two variables, response latency (to items in the role play) and social skill (which was defined as making requests, resisting peer pressure, and being emphatic). The investigators reported the following reliabilities for the variables of response latency and social skills, respectively: internal consistency, .88 and .76; test-retest, .02 and .67; and inter-observer reliability, .82 and .97. Moreover, validities also differ. Content validity is appraised qualitatively by expert opinion. The forms of empirical validity, concurrent, predictive, and construct, bear no logical relationship to each other. One would expect the highest correlations to be obtained in concurrent validity, since measurements are taken at the same point in time. Correspondingly, the lowest correlations should occur in construct validity, since the relationships are abstract and possibly more indirect.

Interobserver reliability and content validity are very closely related, since they both rely on expert judgment and opinion. Furthermore, they are also strongly related in their verbal contents. However, inter-observer reliability as well as internal consistency are not necessarily related to the various kinds of empirical validity; they may be more related to concurrent validity and less related to those types of validity that require predictions across time. Test-retest reliability is more likely to be related to predictive and construct validity than to concurrent validity. These speculations about the relationship between reliability and validity indicate that the relationship is complex. As a result, it is advisable to regard reliability and validity as separate phenomena and not necessarily related. Hence, one should not assume that a particular type of reliability or validity occurs unless there is evidence for it.

CHARACTERISTICS OF USEFUL VARIABLES

Descriptions of variables and their inter-relationships are products of the measuring process. Variables can be employed to gain a better understanding of the nature of clients' problems and to gauge the progress of clients in different phases of practice. They form the keystone of empirically based practice.

Toward this end, it is important to identify characteristics of useful variables. In general, useful variables are those variables that provide information that is pertinent to practice tasks and decisions. Useful variables should be relevant, reliable, valid, sensitive, and cost-efficient.

To be relevant, information derived from variables should relate to practice objectives and their realization in the different phases of practice. In this way, they are more likely to be applicable to social work tasks, decisions, and functions. Suppose, for instance, that a social worker has been asked to work with an in-patient psychiatric client who is refusing to take antipsychotic medication. Data yielded by a measurement tool suggests that the client has inaccurate information about the side-effects of the medication and that the relationship with the doctor prescribing the medication is weak. This type of information is useful to the worker because it suggests points of intervention.

Useful variables should be reliable and valid, providing relatively accurate measures of the phenomena in which social workers are interested. Although it is not possible to have perfect reliability and validity because of the possible errors that affect the measurement process, it is desirable to use those variables for which there is some rationale and evidence for validity and reliability. As much as is possible within the framework of a given case, social workers should attempt to increase the reliability and validity of variables as they develop and administer measurement tools. The more reliable and valid the information, the more dependable and accurate will be judgments based on it.

Sensitivity of variables refers to the number of values of a variable that can be reliably discriminated. In a nominal scale, the reliable discrimination of 3 categories is more sensitive than the reliable discrimination of 2 categories. For the variable *race,* the categories of "white," "black," or "other minority" provide more information than the categories "white," and "nonwhite." Further specification of the "other minority" category will provide even more information. Reliable, ordinal scales are more sensitive than nominal scales, because they are able to discriminate order between categories as well as the categories themselves. Interval and ratio scales are most sensitive. The key ideas in sensitivity are reliable discrimination and the number of categories or values of a variable. A rating scale for anxiety with 10 levels (or values) is not more sensitive than a rating scale with 3 levels, unless there is evidence that the client can reliably discriminate among these 10 levels. The notion of sensitivity is especially important when a social worker is seeking to measure change on a particular variable. If the variable is not sufficiently sensitive, it may not be able to register change. For example, if one is interested in change of an elderly, invalid client's attitude toward a home health aide from unfriendly to friendly, a reliable scale registering degrees of friendliness and unfriendliness is much more likely to show change than one which only has two values for the attitude, friendly or unfriendly. A variable is cost-efficient if its measurement is obtained relatively inexpensively in a short period of time. The tool or instrument to gather data should be understandable, relatively easy to use, and not too costly in terms of time involved to gather information as well as costs for protocols, equipment, forms, scoring, and data processing.

TYPES OF MEASUREMENT TOOLS

Measurement tools are instruments for gathering data, which can be categorized into one or more variables. Although this section does not describe completely the process and the technical details involved in constructing questionnaires, interview schedules, rating scales, observational forms, and other measurement tools, it is useful to consider instrument types by their structure and ways in which information is gathered. For more comprehensive descriptions of instrument construction, the reader is referred to books by the following authors: Bloom and Fischer, 1982; Corcoran and Fischer, 1987; Grinnell, 1985; and Tripodi and Epstein, 1980.

Basic ways to obtain information from clients are: (1) ask them directly; (2) provide them with forms that ask certain questions; (3) ask significant others who know or have opinions about them; (4) observe them; or (5) obtain information that is already recorded about them. Within each of these sources, forms are employed for recording and processing information. The way in which information is organized varies from structured to unstructured. The information that is structured is categorized into a level of measurement. For example, an answer to a question in a questionnaire may be "yes" or "no," which is a structure for nominal scale measurement. Unstructured responses would be narrative types of information that are not yet classified by a level of measurement. A question such as "How do you feel today?" can elicit a variety of responses, including "fine," "terrible," "great," "why are you asking me?," "how do you feel?," "what do you mean?," or a lengthy description of an unpleasant experience that occurred earlier in the day.

Instruments for asking questions directly in face-to-face verbal exchanges are interview schedules. *Structured* interviews involve the direct questioning of a respondent by an interviewer. The questions and possible client responses are fixed in structure, order, and content. Every respondent is asked the same questions and asked to choose among the response alternatives that are given. In *unstructured* interviews, the contents, structure, and order of questions vary depending on the responses of clients and how much detail is sought by probing. *Focused* or *semistructured* interviews contain a fixed set of themes and possibly some questions within them. Responses to structured interviews are recorded on interview schedules; those to semistructured or unstructured interviews are preserved by videotape or audiotape or the interviewer may take notes during or after the interview.

Questionnaires, rating scales, tests of ability, knowledge, and achievement, and projective tests are instruments that can be used without direct face-to-face interactions between an interviewer and a respondent. Rating scales are structured. Questionnaires and tests of ability, knowledge, and achievement are mostly structured, but can contain unstructured items (open-ended questions). Projective tests tend to be unstructured with regard to possible responses, but have structured scoring systems to categorize the responses. Projective tests are much more complicated to use and interpret; they require a background in psychological testing, psychological theory, and psychometrics. This is especially true for administering and interpreting protocols, such as the TAT, sentence completion tests, and the Rorschach. For a basic understanding of psychological testing, the reader is referred to Anastasi's handbook (Anastasi, 1976).

All of these instruments assume a relatively high degree of literacy in the respondents. These instruments can be administered to groups of clients as well as individual clients. Questionnaires and rating scales might also be sent by mail to clients' homes. Questionnaires contain instructions for responding and a series of questions or statements that can be categorized into various measurement levels. For example, an ordinal level of measurement on a questionnaire might include a rating scale such as: To what extent do you agree or disagree with the following statement?

It is impossible to change my attitude toward my boss.
__strongly agree, __agree, __disagree, __strongly disagree

Questionnaires can contain rating scales as well as questions with other alternatives such as:

How many times did you take a dose of pain medication today?
__0, __1, __2, __3, __4, __5 or more

An instrument can be comprised solely of rating scales or it might consist of only one scale. For example, a client might be asked to record his degree of anxiety every morning after rising and every evening before going to bed on a scale such as this:

How anxious do you feel now?
__not at all anxious, __slightly anxious, __very anxious,
__flooded with anxiety

To some extent, the type of information being sought will suggest certain formats for instruments. When seeking information about a client's ability, knowledge, or achievement, the instrument often contains questions with responses that are true-false, multiple-choice, or that require an exact answer. If used widely, the tests may be standardized so that average norms are available for different populations and subpopulations.

To obtain information about client moods or attitudes, clients need to be queried directly. Interviews also are useful when dealing with clients who may not be literate in the language of the question, whether because of vocabulary, syntax, or custom. Questionnaires are preferred for literate individuals. Clients can be trained to use simple rating scales to rate themselves or others on prescribed dimensions.

Although clients might be able to provide information on their own behavior, obtaining information through observation is most valid. Nonparticipant observation in which the observer (such as the social worker) is not interacting with an observee (such as the client) is more accurate than participant observation. The social worker working with a client is a participant observer. So long as the interactions do not involve a great deal of feelings of the worker for the client, the worker's observations may be relatively unbiased. If there is over- or under-identification with the client or countertransference type reactions, however, the observations may be distorted.

Observations involve either visual and/or audio information. There may be live observations or observations of a live event that are preserved by videotape. The social worker may be the observer, as well as the worker's supervisor or a colleague. The client or a member of the client system, such as a family member, may also be an observer. Instruments used for observation are forms for recording, which may include instructions pertaining to which type of data to attend to, and where observations are to take place, and how to record observations.

Observational forms may include rating scales as well as space for counting the frequencies of certain events. For example, in a family interview with the father, teenage son, and mother, the worker might be interested in observing the number and type of interactions that are initiated by the son and the parents. Figure 2.1 illustrates a recording form the worker might use to monitor a family's ability to use certain skills (such as active listening) and avoid certain communications (such as lectures or antagonizing remarks). The form also contains rating scales to capture the worker's general impressions of the family's communication and negotiation skills.

Date of Observation: _____

Observer: _____

Family members present:

Topic being discussed:

	Father	Mother	Son
Frequency of:			
Blaming statements or accusations			
Antagonizing statements			
Lectures			
Positive statements			
Suggested compromises			
Active listening			

Overall ability of family to express thoughts and feelings without alienating others

1	2	3	4	5
No ability; completely alienating		Alienate other members about 1/2 of time		High ability to express thoughts and feelings; rarely alienates others

Overall ability of family to negotiate compromises

1	2	3	4	5
Never reach compromise		Some ability to negotiate compromise		Can negotiate compromise most of time

Figure 2.1 Form for Recording Observation of Family Interaction

Significant others can be provided with questionnaires or rating scales or they can be interviewed to provide information about a particular client family or group. Of course, such information should be confidential and should be obtained in an ethical manner that protects a client's rights and is in accordance with the policies of the agency for which the social worker is employed.

In many instances, data have already been accumulated about the client in places such as school, employment, health and welfare, and other institutions. Information from these sources may be in archival records, such as attendance information in school and performance ratings in employment. Hence, for a child who has difficulty in school, there may be data regarding number of days absent, number of days tardy, percentage of homework assignments completed, number of times referred to principal for disciplinary actions, and grades. Again, care must be taken to follow ethical procedures and to protect client confidentiality when securing such information.

REPEATED MEASUREMENT AND CHANGE

As the basic tool for gathering information about variables, instruments must be administered in a manner that is impartial, confidential, and ethical. When repeated measurements of a variable are to be taken, they must be administered systematically and rigorously. In other words, the instruments must be completed according to the intended procedures or directions and under the same circumstances, at each administration. This is to ensure, to the extent possible, that biases are minimized and that any influences apparent in the measurement process are relatively constant.

The basic purposes for obtaining repeated measurement of a variable from a particular instrument are:

1. To provide evidence for test-retest reliability.
2. To observe whether changes take place.
3. To determine the extent to which there is change.

Test-retest reliability requires two measurements spaced over time. The interval between measures should be clinically meaningful in relation to the particular variables being measured. For example, if one were interested in observing symptoms of severe depression on a daily basis, the time interval between measurements should be one day. On the other hand, the time interval should not be so short that responses are not likely to change due to the respondent's memory and the possible attempt to be consistent. This is especially problematic for tests of knowledge and questionnaires about client attitudes that contain very few items. With these types of instruments, an adequate period of time might be two weeks.

More than two measurements are necessary to observe whether changes occur and whether they are persistent. After one is satisfied that there is a sufficient degree of reliability, one can then take repeated measures to determine whether there can be change. But what is change? *Change* refers to a reliable difference in values of a variable over two or more points in time. The reason the variables must be reliable is to eliminate the possibility that the "change" is simply an artifact due to undesirability or error in the measurement system. A *shift in value* refers to different categories. For example, in a nominal scale that reflects presence or absence of certain behaviors, change is evident when there is a shift from presence to absence or from absence to presence. *Positive change* is sometimes used to refer to a shift that is made in a clinically desirable direction. Hence, a shift from presence of obsessive-compulsive behaviors to absence of obsessive-compulsive behaviors could be construed as *positive change;* absence to presence of symptoms as *negative change;* and no shifts in value as *no change.*

The preceding definition of change is sufficient for the nominal scale of measurement, but may not be for ordinal and interval-ratio measurement scales. With these measurement scales, the definition of change also requires a statement about the magnitude of change. Suppose there is an interval scale for counting the number of flashbacks experienced by a rape victim in one day. Further, suppose the rape victim experiences 20 flashbacks on one day, followed by 19, 20, 15, 5, and 4 flashbacks per day on successive days. Change might be defined as any change in level; hence there would be changes in the level of flashbacks every day. But that might not be meaningful to the worker and client since flashbacks (and presumably emotional trauma) are still reflected in the measures. A different definition might indicate that change occurs when there is a sufficient change in level so that it can be construed as clinically significant in relation to the goals of treatment. For example, change might be regarded as occurring only if there is a reduction of flashbacks by 75%; thus, change would only be evident when the client drops from 20 flashbacks per day to 5 flashbacks per day. Of course, some clinicians may regard change as occurring only when there are no flashbacks whatsoever, and this would be an instance where a nominal scale of flashbacks or no flashbacks is preferred. Still another definition would involve the use of statistical reasoning. First, one would calculate an average number of flashbacks for a prescribed time interval, such as 20 flashbacks a day for 3 days. Second, one would set a level of statistical significance. For example, in subsequent observations change is only evident if the number of flashbacks is consistently below the average of 20 at a probability of less than 5 times out of 100.

In summary, *change* refers to reliable shifts in level. The shifts can be at any level, or there may be further criteria imposed such as clinical and/or statistical significance.

Once there is an agreed on definition of change by worker and client, the extent to which there is stability in the variable over time can be determined. Repeated measurements enable the social worker to learn whether there is a problem and whether it persists. Depending on the type of measurement scale used and the definition of change employed, one could also determine the extent to which the problem persists. For example, a client may exhibit a high level of flashbacks, and there are no changes in that level over time. For a particular client, a social worker may not be so much interested in positive change, but in avoiding the occurrence of negative changes if the goals are preventive. Hence, a stable low level of flashbacks is desirable, and a negative change would be undesirable with respect to the social worker's treatment goals.

MULTIPLE MEASUREMENT

Multiple measurement involves the use of two or more variables measured simultaneously. There are two possibilities for such measurement: (1) measuring multiple variables of the same concept; or (2) measuring multiple variables that represent different concepts for the same client or client system.

Multiple variables of the same concept build in validation of the variables, and provide the potential advantage of increasing confidence in the results when there is consistency in them. For example, the concept may be anxiety. This could be measured in one way by the self-report of the client on a paper-and-pencil test of anxiety, such as the State-Trait Anxiety Inventory (Spielberger, Gorsuch, & Lushene, 1970). Another measurement procedure might include ratings of the client by significant others on scales of anxiety. Still another variable might entail the use of a physiological measurement device such as heart rate. These three variables are indices of anxiety, but no one variable captures the essence of the concept. If all three variables are reliable and they are intercorrelated, showing consistent changes in relation to client objectives, then there is increased evidence for validity. Consistent changes would be indicated if a client was high on anxiety on the three measures before treatment or intervention and low on anxiety after treatment. If there are not consistent results, then one can only discuss change, if and as it occurs, for each variable. The variable that would be most useful is the one that more closely is pertinent to worker-client objectives. In the above example, if the client described anxiety as hyperventilating and a racing pulse, the heart rate might be the most appropriate and valid measure of change.

Variables representing different concepts may also be obtained for a client who has multiple goals. For example, a client may wish to improve her self-image, increase the number of positive interactions with her spouse, and spend more time with her children. Different information would be collected to monitor change in each variable. If there are consistent, desirable changes across all three variables, there is validation of the treatment or intervention. There still is partial validation even if only one or two of the variables show change.

Measuring multiple variables can be useful for purposes of validation and for providing different views about the results of intervention. Because it is costly, however, workers should collect only those data that are reflective of client and worker objectives.

SELECTING AVAILABLE INSTRUMENTS

It is most efficient to use instruments or tools that are already available for purposes of obtaining measurements of variables, if these instruments are judged to be valid indicators of change in terms of the goals of treatment for a particular client. As previously indicated, instruments may appear in many forms: questionnaires, interview schedules, objective tests, projective tests, observational forms, personality inventories, agency fact sheets, and sentence completion tests, to name the most common examples. An instrument may be unidimensional, with all of its items reflecting one variable, or it may be multidimensional, with many different variables, as in an agency fact sheet that might collect such information as gender, age, family composition, and previous mental health treatment. Instruments are available in source books (see, for example, Aero & Weiner, 1981; Corcoran & Fischer, 1987; Hudson, 1982), in manuals at research agencies and institutes, from publishers of psychological tests, and from individual authors of tests.

To choose instruments, the following criteria, modified and adapted from Tripodi and Epstein (1980) might be helpful: practicality, purpose, minimal measurement errors, reliability, validity, and availability of norms. *Practicality* refers to the length of time it takes to complete instruments, the degree to which they are understandable, their costs, and the amount of training necessary to use them. Instruments should be understandable. Those that do not require training can be used immediately. For most purposes, they should be relatively short, requiring less than a half hour to complete. Some instruments take as little as 1-2 minutes to complete. If the resulting information is reliable, valid, and sufficient to facilitate practice decision making, such brevity is acceptable and desirable.

In considering available instruments, the intended purposes of the instrument should be considered. For instance, some instruments are only intended for screening or for diagnosis, and would not be appropriate for repeated application to assess client change. Instruments may also vary in terms of the type of information collected — quantitative or qualitative. Obviously, the worker must be specific about the kind of information that is desired before instruments can be evaluated in terms of purpose.

Instruments that contain a substantial amount of measurement error should be used with caution. Workers should look for biases in the instructions and consider the extent to which biases may be present in the measuring environment and in the predispositions of clients, workers themselves, or others who complete or use the instrument.

Instruments should contain content validity and the appropriate type of reliability for the variables being measured. If the variable(s) measured by the instrument are not valid in terms of the particular goals for this client, the information collected will be of limited help. Similarly, information that is highly unreliable cannot be used with any degree of confidence.

Some instruments contain norms for key variables. *Norms* are average measures of a specific population for the specific variable under consideration. For example, there are average scores on reading and intelligence tests. Or, there may be average standardized scores on a checklist of child behavior problems for institutionalized children. Workers should look for a description of the population on which the norms were based, paying special attention to demographic characteristics such as age, gender, and social class. If the client is clearly a member of the subpopulation from which the norms are developed, and if the subpopulation is representative of clients like the individual currently being seen, then the norms might be employed to locate the extent to which this particular client is above, below, or at the average level with regard to a specific variable of interest.

EXERCISES

1. Select a concept such as depression and operationally define it.
2. (a) Devise a rating scale that you could use to describe the extent to which a member of a couple (or a family or group) to whom you are providing services and/or intervention is involved in a treatment session.

    (b) Devise a test for measuring the interobserver reliability of this rating scale and perform the reliability test with hypothetical scores, using percentage agreement as the index of reliability.

    (c) Discuss how the scale might be validated by content and empirical validity.

3. Locate or devise variables pertinent to our practice that are in these measurement forms: (a) nominal scale; (b) ordinal scale; (c) interval scale.

4. Describe two variables from your practice that represent each of the types:
    (a) Type 1 — client characteristics observed by significant others;
    (b) Type 2 — client moods, feelings, attitudes, beliefs, and values;
    (c) Type 3 — knowledge, ability, and achievement;
    (d) Type 4 — observable client behavior.

5. Describe and give examples, reflective of your practice, of the following types of reliability and validity:
    (a) test-retest reliability
    (b) split-half reliability
    (c) predictive validity
    (d) concurrent validity

6. Select an available instrument that is used or could be used in your practice.
    (a) Identify one variable from the instrument.
    (b) Discuss the extent to which there are measurement errors in producing data for this variable.
    (c) Discuss the advantages and disadvantages of using that instrument for the measurement of this variable.

7. Discuss the extent to which you believe variables can be created or located that show client change as identified in your practice.

Chapter 3

ASSESSMENT

PURPOSE OF ASSESSMENT

Assessment is of critical importance in social work practice. Its purpose is to identify and locate the extent and nature of potential client problems. It sets the stage for major decisions affecting direct practice and provides information for answering such questions as: Does a potential client satisfy the conditions of eligibility in a particular agency or system of agencies? Should the client be referred to other agencies? Is there a problem that requires a solution?

The amount of time that can be devoted to assessment varies by type and function of agency. In Traveler's Aid, for example, assessment and other phases of practice occur in a very brief encounter in which services are provided in relation to need: travel arrangements, financial assistance, shelter, location of significant others, and so forth. On the other hand, institutional settings allow workers to accumulate much more information for the determination of client treatment and services. Our approach in this chapter is to assume there is sufficient time for assessment, especially since facts and inferences made in that stage are crucial in such work as protective services, mental health hospitals, child welfare, and family service agencies. Nonetheless, the assessment should not be prolonged unnecessarily.

In assessment, the worker attempts to make an inventory of potential client problems, and of the strengths, weaknesses, and resources the client possesses. The client's behaviors, cognitions, and feelings with respect to the target problems are identified, and the conditions under which problems occur are specified.

PROBLEM-FOCUSED ASSESSMENT

Since much of practice is based on a problem-solving perspective, it is important to consider what is meant by a *problem*. We use the term broadly to refer to something the client and/or worker perceives as troubling to the client and/or the client's significant others. *Problem* in this sense incorporates the notion of basic human needs. Problem resolution may require change in the problem itself, in attitudes and feelings about the problem, or in the conditions under which the problem occurs. In an instance of child abuse by the child's mother, for example, the problem may be identified as the physical beating of the child, regardless of whether the mother perceives it as a problem. Or the problem may be identified as the mother's inability to perceive the action toward the child as abusive.

Clients are more likely to initially define problems in voluntary social agencies when contacts between social workers and clients are not mandatory, such as family service agencies, mental health agencies, medical hospitals, and community organizations. In nonvoluntary agencies, both workers and clients may define problems. Services in protective services, correctional facilities, and public mental hospitals are not typically initiated by the clients, but occur in response to problems defined by the community. For either type of agency, voluntary or nonvoluntary, it is important in assessment to delineate the problems in terms of the perceptions of worker, client, and significant others, for these similarities or differences in problem perception may be predictive of the extent to which an intervention might be successfully implemented. If worker, client, and significant others agree in their perceptions of the problem, there is likely to be a greater degree of worker-client cooperation and rapport.

INFORMATION FOR ASSESSMENT

As indicated previously in Chapter 2, there are four major types of information that are relevant to assessment: Type 1, the client characteristics that can be observed by significant others, social workers, and clients; Type 2, client's moods, feelings, attitudes, beliefs, and values; Type 3, knowledge, ability, and achievement; Type 4, observable behaviors of clients. Typical information that might be collected within each category of this typology is discussed below.

Type 1. Major amounts of information are provided in the form of Type 1 variables. The actual information collected depends on such things as client problems, worker's theoretical orientation, and agency setting. In addition to basic information describing socioeconomic and demographic variables of clients, Type 1 information may include diagnostic categories and environmental information, as two examples.

Diagnostic classifications are provided by systems such as the *Diagnostic and Statistical Manual of Mental Disorders* (1980), which contains a categorical system for diagnosing mental disorders, and represents a first step in assessment of mental disorders. Commonly referred to as DSM-III, the following diagnostic categories are included in the manual: disorders usually first evident in infancy, childhood, or adolescence, organic mental disorders, substance use disorders, schizophrenic disorders; paranoid disorders, psychotic disorders not elsewhere classified, affective disorders, anxiety disorders, somatic disorders, dissociative disorders, psychosexual disorders, factitious disorders, disorders of impulse control, adjustment disorders, personality disorders, and psychological factors affecting physical conditions. As pointed out in the manual, workers with different theoretical orientations (such as psychodynamic, behavioral, or family therapy) would require more detailed assessments relevant to those perspectives. The manual includes information related to five axes: clinical syndromes; personality and developmental disorders; physical disorders and conditions; severity of psychosocial stressors; and highest level of adaptive functioning in the past year. Information from DSM-III is likely to be used in mental health and some family service and child guidance agencies. Social workers may not make the diagnoses themselves, but they might use such information in their assessments. In so doing, it is advisable that the measurement concepts of reliability and validity be invoked. In Appendix F (p. 470) of the Manual, some interrater reliability coefficients are provided. For example, there was greater reliability in rating syndromes of organic mental disorders (Kappa = .79) than in paranoid disorders (Kappa = .66). Robins and Helzer (1986) provide a critique of the structure of DSM-III and information regarding reliability and validity of different parts of the classification system. It is important to recognize that the system is not completely accurate and that reliability and validity varies by different categories. Moreover, there is not a great deal of information pertaining to the system's reliability and validity. Nevertheless, it is used worldwide and it does provide a designation with descriptions of psychiatric syndromes now in use.

Type 1 information frequently focuses on the client in relationship to his or her environment. Measures of social supports or family ties may be collected. For example, family therapists and child welfare workers often use the ecomap, which helps to identify sources of informal and formal social supports, losses (of important relationships or supports), and stressful relationships/situations. The worker shows strong, tenuous, or stressful connections, where they exist, between the family and other areas in their environment. The completed ecomap (Figure 3.1), adapted from Hartman (1982), expresses the social supports, resources, and stressors for a family who adopted an 8-year-old boy.

Type 2. Client self-rating scales and problem inventories are tools directly related to the assessment of client problems. A number of these tools that are useful for social work direct practice are located in Magura and Moses (1986) and in Corcoran and Fischer (1987). Magura and Moses describe and provide a number of instruments that contain variables related to the assessment of children and families. For example, their manual catalogs the Behavior Problem Checklist, which identifies types and degrees of behavior problems experienced by children. It also presents the Child Well-Being Scales, a set of 43 items pertaining to topics such as: physical safety in the home, parental consistency in discipline, sexual abuse, and school attendance.

Corcoran and Fischer's book contains numerous paper-and-pencil questionnaires, rating scales, and problem inventories related to specific client concerns such as stressful situations, assertion problems, and family conflict. It contains a number of relatively reliable and valid instruments that measure a range of attitudes, moods, cognitions, and behaviors: marital adjustment, self-concept, family relationships, guilt, depression, anxiety, to name a few examples. Under marital adjustment, to further illustrate, is Hudson's Index of Marital Satisfaction presented in Figure 3.2 (Hudson, 1982). Corcoran and Fischer provide guidelines for scoring and interpreting each instrument, reliability and validity information, and a reference to a paper discussing the instrument.

Type 3. Information about standardized knowledge and achievement tests is available in O. K. Buros's (1978) *The Eighth Mental Measurements Yearbook,* the classic reference work for psychological tests. Each test is described and information about its reliability and validity is provided. If necessary, however, new tests of knowledge can easily be developed. For example, a worker may be interested in the client's knowledge of the effects of a particular medication being prescribed to the client. The worker can devise an objective test containing true-false and multiple-choice items to assess the client's knowledge of both intended and possible side-effects of the drug. Also useful for assess-

ECO-MAP*

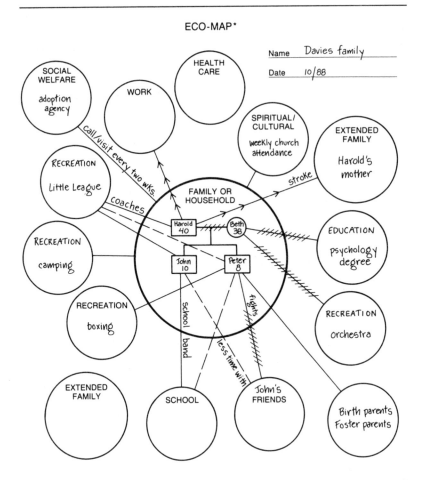

Fill in connections where they exist. Indicate nature of connections with a descriptive word or by drawing different kinds of lines: ———— for strong, — — — — for tenuous, /////// for stressfull. Draw arrows along lines to signify flow of energy, resources and so forth. Identify significant people and fill in empty circles as needed.

* Adapted from Hartman (1982)

Figure 3.1

ment are tests of achievement and ability. Tests of reading comprehension, vocabulary, and mechanical aptitude are examples of the types of tests that can be developed by social workers.

Type 4. Basic kinds of information for these types of variables are observations that can be made by clients, social workers or other

INDEX OF MARITAL SATISFACTION (IMS)*   Today's Date _____

NAME_____

This questionnaire is designed to measure the degree of satisfaction you have with your present marriage. It is not a test, so there are no right or wrong answers. Answer each item as carefully and as accurately as you can by placing a number beside each one as follows:

> 1 Rarely or none of the time
> 2 A little of the time
> 3 Some of the time
> 4 A good part of the time
> 5 Most or all of the time

Please begin.

1	I feel that my partner is affectionate enough.	___
2	I feel that my partner treats me badly.	___
3	I feel that my partner really cares for me.	___
4	I feel that I would not choose the same partner if I had it to do over again.	___
5	I feel that I can trust my partner.	
6	I feel that our relationship is breaking up.	___
7	I feel that my partner doesn't understand me.	___
8	I feel that our relationship is a good one.	___
9	I feel that ours is a very happy relationship.	
10	I feel that our life together is dull.	___
11	I feel that we have a lot of fun together.	___
12	I feel that my partner doesn't confide in me.	___
13	I feel that ours is a very close relationship.	___
14	I feel that I cannot rely on my partner.	___
15	I feel that we do not have enough interests in common.	___
16	I feel that we manage arguments and disagreements very well.	___
17	I feel that we do a good job of managing our finances.	___
18	I feel that I should have never married my partner.	___
19	I feel that my partner and I get along very well together.	___
20	I feel that our relationship is very stable.	
21	I feel that my partner is a comfort to me.	___
22	I feel that I no longer care for my partner.	___
23	I feel that the future looks bright for our relationship.	___
24	I feel that our relationship is empty.	___
25	I feel there is no excitement in our relationship.	___

Copyright © The Dorsey Press, 1982

1,3,5,8,9,11,13,16,17,19,20,21,23

*Hudson (1982)

Figure 3.2

professionals, and/or significant others. Most often, forms for counting the frequency and duration of behaviors are developed with respect to a specific client behavior. To initially identify behaviors for assessment, one can employ a problem inventory. For instance, one could use the Self-Rating Behavior Scale, which consists of 73 problematic behaviors (Upper & Cautela, 1975). Clients check each behavior they think they need to learn. Each checked item is discussed with the client; if worker and client agree to try to change that behavior, the worker can then devise an observational device to assess the extent of the problem and to monitor the client's progress in changing that behavior. Not all of the 73 behaviors are overt (that is, able to be observed by someone other than the client). An example of an item that can only be assessed by the client is: "to feel less anxious about being alone." Obviously, only overt behaviors can be observed, such as "to stop biting my fingernails," "to stop wetting the bed at night," "to hold down a steady job," or "to stop swearing at other people." If, for example, the client checks "to stop swearing at other people," the worker and client would agree on an operational definition of swearing and then devise a way in which information could be provided on the extent of the problem. Suppose the client says that where he really swears too much and inappropriately is at work, where he conducts training sessions on sales. Swearing may be defined as using four-letter word expletives. An observer (significant other or colleague, for example) could count the number of four-letter word expletives used during his training sessions. Or the lectures could be tape recorded and the worker and client could independently count the number of expletives and determine the extent to which their counts are reliable. In this instance, the form would be a simple sheet listing the behavior, data, type of class session, and tallies for the number of times the expletives occurred.

Another observation but one that only the client can measure was used by Berlin (1978) in her research on self-criticism among women. She developed a form, depicted in Figure 3.3, in which the client records self-criticisms within specific categories. The operational definitions of self-criticisms are contained in the self-monitoring instructions.

DECIDING WHAT TYPE OF INFORMATION TO GATHER

Workers should consider multiple factors when deciding on the amounts and types of information to gather, including the purposes of the assessment, the information already available, the certainty in existing assessments, time available for assessment, priority of assess-

SUGGESTED CATEGORIES FOR MONITORING SELF-CRITICISM*

Name _____

Date _____

TIME	10:00	11:00	12:00	1:00	2:00	3:00	4:00	5:00	6:00	7:00	8:00	9:00	10:00
1. Overeating													
2. Physical Appearance													
3. Negative Comparisons													
4. Undisciplined/Disorganized													
5. Lazy/Nonproductive													
6. Immature/Infantile													
7. Unintelligent													
8. Indecisive													
9. Unassertive													
10. Too Aggressive													
11. Irresponsible													
12. Selfish													
13. Jealous													
14. Incompetent													
15. Other													

*Berlin, S.B. An investigation of the effects of cognitive-behavior modification treatments on problems of inappropriate self-criticism among women. Unpublished doctoral dissertation, University of Washington, 1978.

Figure 3.3

SELF-MONITORING INSTRUCTIONS

1   On the hour from 10 a.m. to 10 p.m., reflect back on the previous hour and determine
     whether you have self-criticized during that time.

2   If you have, make a mark in the cell formed by the intersection of the *time* period in
     which the criticism occurred and the *type* (category) of self-criticism.

3   A self-criticism is any negative thought that you have about yourself. It is the same
     as blaming yourself, feeling guilty, negatively evaluating yourself, or expecting the
     worst of yourself. Self-criticism can be brief, e.g., "dummy!", or it can last for an
     extended period of time – it is not uncommon for a person to mull over her "inade-
     quacy" in a given situation for hours.

4   For purposes of recording, criticism associated with one event (one type) is counted
     as one criticism unless the criticism lasts or recurs for more than one hour. If a
     criticism around a single event extends beyond one hour, record the criticism in both
     hours; if it extends into three hours, record it three times.

5   If you criticize yourself for several different reasons during one hour, mark those
     reasons under the same hour.

6   It is preferable to observe and record your self-criticisms in this manner every day
     for the next seven days. But seven days is a long time. If something comes up and
     you can't record during one day (or you can't make yourself record one more day),
     take a day off. *ACCURACY IS BETTER THAN QUANTITY.* When you self-observe,
     do it hourly according to the instructions. When you need a break, take a whole day
     off. You can take up to three days "vacation" per week if you need it.

7   You will be a more efficient observer if you make it a point to observe – to stay in
     tune with how you are feeling and what you are thinking about yourself. It may be
     helpful to ask yourself from time to time, "How am I feeling now?" Some people
     may negatively evaluate themselves in highly articulate forms, other people may use
     images, others may bypass words and images and get immediately into feeling badly.
     Whichever pattern you tend to follow, try to put the criticism into words. A shift in
     feeling to a sense of feeling distressed may be a cue that you have been negatively
     evaluating yourself. When you notice that you are feeling sad or upset with yourself,
     review what your specific thoughts are or were.

8   Keep the check-list with you all of the time.

Figure 3.3 (Continued)

ment, severity of problems, whether additional information is needed
to determine client eligibility, and the worker's orientation to practice.
     First, workers need to consider why an assessment is being done.
There may be very specific types of information demanded by the

agency, which, in turn, is required by agency sponsors. The assessment may provide information from which worker and client will select target problems to address in treatment. Or, the assessment may provide additional information to that which is already available for purposes of assessing validity. The purpose of the assessment provides a frame of reference regarding the degree to which potential information is relevant.

Second, workers should determine the extent to which information is already available. The client may have been referred from other agencies and some information may have been provided. Or the client may previously have been a client at this agency. The available information, however, may be unreliable and invalid. Considering the extent to which the information is reliable and valid will help the worker achieve the third step, which is to decide on the degree of certainty about existing assessments.

If there is reliable and valid information that is relevant to the purpose of assessment, the worker may decide that existing assessments, if available, are sufficient. On the other hand, the social worker may be uncertain about some types of information, and may seek to verify these data in an interview with the client.

Time available for assessment is the fourth criterion, and a practical one. Is there sufficient time and client availability, as well as worker availability, to make an assessment? This factor is coupled with the notion of agency priorities. If workers are extremely busy and involved with other problematic situations, how much priority is there for an assessment of a particular client? Priority, in part, is determined by apparent severity of client problems. If a client is referred to an agency or if the client voluntarily dropped in, a prime consideration is the extent to which the agency needs information to determine eligibility. For example, verification of financial need might be required if financial assistance is to be offered.

In general, the amount of time available to make an assessment is important in determining how much information will be gathered. If there appears to be multiple problems and/or needs, the assessment usually requires more information than cases for which there is a single specific, time-limited problem. Relevancy to the purpose of the assessment and the worker's orientation to practice are crucial for determining the specific types of information to gather from the four types of data. A psychodynamically oriented worker may gather data from interviews and from instruments that provide Type 2 data (i.e., information on moods, attitudes, and feelings). A cognitively oriented worker might emphasize data from Type 4 on observations as well as Type 2 data. A school social worker may be interested in Type 3 data on knowledge and achievement. A behavioral worker may focus on Type 4 data. Type 1 data would be important for all agency workers.

REDUCING BIASES IN ASSESSMENT

To increase the accuracy of assessment, it is important to be aware of potential errors and biases, and to be vigilant in attempting to reduce these errors. Workers should consider the context in which assessments are made, possible errors when a single instrument is used to gather information, and the problem of processing information when multiple sources of data and/or instruments are employed.

The context of assessment includes such dimensions as the physical location of assessment, constraints on the amounts and types of information to be gathered, time limitations, and the agency's function and purpose. Just as the measuring environment was regarded in Chapter 2 as a potential source of error in the use of an instrument, so it is also influential in terms of the agency context for assessment. In emergency situations — such as natural disasters, episodic violence, and family disruption — assessment often takes place quickly and is interwoven with the offer of assistance and crisis intervention. With both worker and client undergoing stress, the possibility of error increases. Agency predispositions and workers' biases may influence assessment decisions. For example, workers in a child protective agency might easily identify with a child and assume that a parent accused of child abuse actually abused his or her child; and be, therefore, careless in gathering and analyzing information. To minimize bias in agency contexts, the social worker should:

1. Attempt to be nonjudgmental when gathering and processing information.
2. If time permits, gather more than one source of information, representing different points of view pertaining to assessment.
3. Examine information with the concepts of reliability and validity in mind.
4. Consider the extent to which there might be predisposing factors in the assessment environment.

When only one measuring device is used for assessment, consider the possible errors and take those into account when rendering assessment decisions. Recall from Chapter 2 that there are potential biases in the format of the instrument and in the instructions, as well as in the measuring environment. The use of a questionnaire in which a client is asked to report symptoms of anxiety can be subject to errors such as these:

1. The assessment environment itself may generate anxiety. As an extreme example, a teenager arrested for the first time, handcuffed, and ignorant of the procedures involved may appear more anxious than he usually is. Even more innocuous assessment environments, such as a clinic office and the presence of a professional social worker, may increase anxiety.
2. The client may not understand the language employed and may provide neutral responses to items, thereby masking his/her true feelings.
3. The cultural traditions of the client's family may not permit her or him to respond accurately to certain items. The young boy may not be allowed to express fear, for example; thus, he would appear less anxious than he actually is.

When more than one instrument is used, there are many potential sources of error. These can be minimized by maintaining an attitude of objectivity and by consciously striving to be impartial. Steps such as the following can be helpful:

1. Examine the reliability and validity of each instrument. Then rank order the instruments from most useful to least useful in assessment.
2. Categorize instruments into those that are based on similar or different assumptions and data-gathering strategies. To illustrate, instruments based on clients' self-reports are similar with respect to data-gathering strategy, while information based on the observations of a significant other are different from a client's self-report.
3. Compare the results of the data from each instrument, looking for consistencies and inconsistencies. For instance, do self-reported child abuse, observations of child abuse by significant others, and abuse reported by the victim all provide a set of consistent data regarding child abuse?
4. When data from different sources are inconsistent, refer to the question of reliability and validity. Make a decision based on the most accurate data or, time permitting, collect additional data.
5. When there are multiple instruments providing data that lead to inconsistent conclusions, another way to reduce potential error, this time in the interpretation of data, is to gather a second opinion. In this way, there is some basis for referring to the reliability of the assessment.

ASSESSING THE EXTENT OF CLIENT PROBLEMS

A client's problem is measurable to the degree that it can be operationalized in the form of variables. Some problems can be operationalized into a single variable such as alcoholism, child abuse, delinquency, psychosis, unemployment, or poverty. Other problems are more complex and may be represented by more than one variable. For example, a "relationship problem" between a couple may lead to a number of different variables, including dissatisfaction with the relationship, number of positive and negative verbal interactions, and frequency of sex.

After having considered the services that the agency provides and the types of clients and problems with which the agency is concerned, the social worker can examine how to operationalize the problem. One way to identify problems is to understand the agency's function and purpose by observing the types of services and the reasons for prioritizing these services. An agency concerned with children and families may provide services to improve family functioning, protect children and spouses, and enable couples to make decisions about continuing their relationships. Services for residents in a home for elderly people may be provided to decrease the feeling of loneliness and to increase their degree of physical comfort, while services provided by a social worker in industry may be to reduce substance abuse by employees.

The key to identifying problems that can be measured is to operationally define variables that can register change or the absence of change. As indicated previously, there can be change as reflected in variables of four different types. Social workers may be interested in reducing or solving problems, in preventing problems from occurring, or in providing care to maintain or to change a client's situation. In any of these events, the specification of variables provides a benchmark for social workers to use in judging the results of their work.

PROBLEM EXISTENCE, MAGNITUDE, DURATION, AND FREQUENCY

There are four basic concepts that can be used for measuring client problems. These concepts are related to the operationalization of variables in terms of measurement scales, and point to phenomena that can remain the same or change over time. These are problem existence, problem magnitude, problem duration, and problem frequency.

Problem existence refers to the presence or absence of a problem. Its simplest form is that of a dichotomous, nominal scale, with one aspect indicating the existence of the problem, and the other nonexistence. The basic ingredient is the operationalization of what constitutes and what does not constitute a problem. For example, a drug abuser might be defined as one who uses any drug that induces physiological and psychological addiction, for other than medical purposes, more than once per week. In defining problem existence, the worker must specify the necessary concepts and give examples regarding how problems and nonproblems should be operationalized. If these specifications are sufficient, interobserver reliability can be demonstrated.

Problem magnitude refers to the intensity, severity, or strength of a problem. It is assessed by employing an ordinal rating scale on which the client, the social worker, and possibly significant others rate the intensity, strength, or severity of the client's problem. The scale itself can include two or more steps and is calibrated so that it is appropriate and relevant to the particular problem being assessed. For example, a scale ranging from 1 as *no problem* to 5 as *a very severe problem* may be used to describe the problem magnitude of an alcoholic teenager as perceived by her father. Or, a scale ranging from 0 to 10 might be used to designate the strength of a client's fear of riding elevators, with 0 representing *no fear at all* to 10 signifying *extreme fear accompanied by physiological symptoms such as sweaty palms, increased heart beat, and feelings of nausea.* The number of points or steps on a scale should be sufficient to distinguish reliably different degrees of the problem, but not so numerous that the client cannot make a distinction between two adjacent points. In general, the scale usually should contain between 3 (for instance, 1 = low, 2 = moderate, 3 = high severity) and 11 points. A 9-point scale might have the following anchors:

1	2	3	4	5	6	7	8	9
Very low severity		Some severity		Moderate severity		High severity		Very high severity

Scales provide more reliable and valid measures of the variable as the anchors become more specific to a particular client's problem. Moreover, the process of developing anchors with the client typically yields some valuable assessment information about the target problem.

Problem duration refers to the length of time that a specified problem occurs from some designated point in time. It is registered on an interval scale of measurement. The unit of time should represent a clinically significant segment of time which, for example, could be days for a students' absence from school, hours for the duration of angry feelings, or minutes for the amount of negative verbal interactions in an interview. Duration can be assessed by the client, social worker, or significant other.

Problem frequency refers to the number of times a problem occurs within a designated time period. It is recorded on a ratio measurement scale. Having defined a problem in such a way that its presence or absence can be identified, the number of times the problem occurs is counted. To count frequencies, however, a reliable observer needs to be in a position to observe the problem. The sexual abuser of a child may be the only person with the child, for example, but the abuser may not report the abuse, and the child may be afraid to tell anyone. Hence, indirect measures such as the presence of bruises, coupled with other information gathered from interviews, might be employed.

GRAPHING INFORMATION RELATED TO CLIENT PROBLEMS

Graphs can be employed to depict variables representing client problems at one or more points in time. Figure 3.4 is a representation of such a graph and its coordinates.

Referring to Figure 3.4, the simple nomenclature used in discussing how graphs are formed will first be presented. The x-axis typically represents time; the time segments are equally divided so that they represent equal time periods. For clinical purposes, the time segments are often days or weeks. The y-axis can be used to represent problem existence, magnitude, duration, or frequency. When problem existence is graphed, 1 signifies existence and 0 indicates nonexistence. If one graphed the occurrence of migraine headaches for a particular client on any given day of a week, it might look like Figure 3.5.

The graph is constructed by plotting a 1 or 0 for each day of the week, depending on whether or not a headache occurred, and then connecting

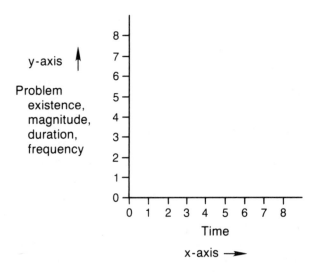

Figure 3.4

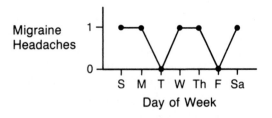

Figure 3.5

the points to form the graph. Figure 3.5 shows that the client experienced a headache every day of the week except Tuesday and Friday.

Problem existence can be treated as problem frequency if it is combined with time. Figure 3.5 depicts 5 days with problems. For any given week, the possible days with problems range from 0 to 7. On another graph, one might represent the number of days a problem exists on a weekly basis. In Figure 3.6, there were 5 days in which the client had migraine headaches in Weeks 1 and 2; 3 days in Weeks 3, 6, 7, and 8; and 2 days in Weeks 4 and 5. The graph in Figure 3.6 was constructed by plotting the coordinates of weeks and number of days with problems for each of the 8 weeks. For example, for Week 3 the client had headaches on 3 days; to plot these coordinates (3,3), go to the appropriate week on the x-axis, 3, and then count on the y-axis from Week 3 the number of days with problems, 3. The point B is the point to be represented on the graph. The coordinates of weeks is represented by line AB, which is the *abscissa;* while the coordinate of number of days with problems is signified by line BC, which is the *ordinate.* All other points on the graph are constructed by plotting the abscissa and ordinate for each week. For example, for week 1 the points are 1,5. Note that the lines AB and BC are not necessary for graphic representation; they are shown here to illustrate the abscissa and ordinate.

When plotting graphs with problem magnitude, employ as many units as are necessary to represent the points used on the scale of magnitude. The points should be equally distant. Time units are again represented on the x-axis. Figure 3.7 shows a graph representing a client's level of self-esteem on a daily basis for a period of 2 weeks. The scale of self-esteem ranges from 1, representing very low self-esteem, to 9, representing high self-esteem. The graph depicts a client whose self-esteem stabilized to a very low level in the second week of observation.

Graphs to represent problem frequency over time are constructed in the same way as graphs representing problem magnitude. However, the numbers along the y-axis representing the frequency with which the problem occurred may have a greater range. For example, the range might surpass 100 when measuring and plotting the number of glasses of beer imbibed by an alcoholic or the number of times one family member swears at another during 1 week.

Note that one or more graphs can be plotted for a client. For instance, two separate graphs might be employed to represent problem frequency and problem magnitude (severity) for the same problem. If a worker has more than one client for which there are similar objectives (such as a marital couple, members in a group, or several clients seen separately but with the same type of problem), several different clients can be

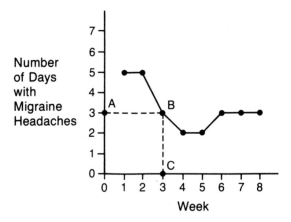

Figure 3.6

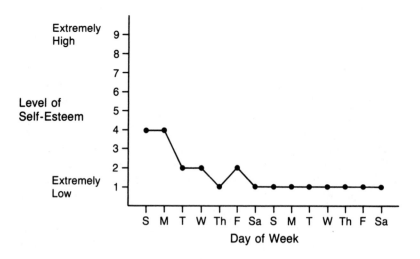

Figure 3.7

represented on the same graph. Figure 3.8 refers to each member of a couple, clients A and B, with respect to their ability to recognize when a discussion is escalating into anger and call for a brief "time out" over a period of 4 weeks. Client A called for many more time outs than client B. Their average use of time outs is also depicted by averaging the ordinates for A and B for each week. Thus, for Week 1, 12 plus 2 divided by 2 equals an average of 7 time outs.

Problem duration can be graphically represented by plotting time on the x-axis as has been done for the graphs above and by specifying a smaller division of time units for each point on the x-axis, employing these units as points on the y-axis. For example, suppose a child has temper tantrums, and one is interested in observing the time spent in temper tantrums (problem duration) as well as the number of tantrums (problem frequency) per day. Two separate graphs can be drawn, one showing frequency and the other, duration. To depict duration, total the time outs (in minutes for this example) for tantrums in each day. That total represents duration, as indicated in Figure 3.9.

To determine the average duration per tantrum over time, simply divide the total duration in minutes by the number of tantrums for a particular day. Suppose there were two tantrums every day for a period of 1 week. In that event, all of the ordinates in Figure 3.9 would be divided by 2, to represent average duration of tantrums. Thus, for Sunday, it would be 25, Monday, 20, Tuesday, 20, and so forth.

Graphs represent pictorially trends over time and show relationships of variables on y-axes to those on x-axes. In Figure 3.10 are some examples of trends that might be observed.

These lines are formed by connecting the ordinates for all time points on the x-axis. Acceleration refers to a trend over time that shows an increase in frequency; in contrast, deceleration refers to a decrease in frequency. Any straight line represents stability, with horizontal stability denoting a line parallel to the x-axis, in which all ordinates are equal. A cyclic pattern refers to a recurring fluctuation in a constant manner, while curvilinear patterns represent curves that follow a consistent, stable pattern, but are nonlinear. In actual practice, there often are combinations of these patterns. For example, the pattern of instances of spouse abuse may be cyclical but accelerating for a given client.

Graphs can be transformed by changing the units on the measurement scales for either the x-axis or the y-axis, or by systematically changing the ordinates to other mathematical functions. These transformations have the purpose of allowing for easier visual interpretations; but if the viewer does not keep in mind what the graphic coordinates are, there is a possibility for distortion, resulting in under- or over-representation of

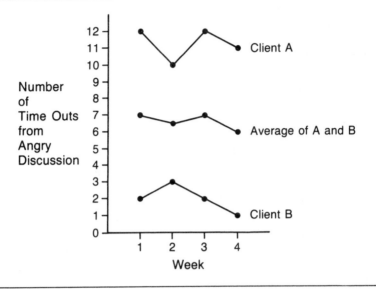

Figure 3.8

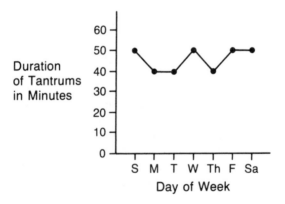

Figure 3.9

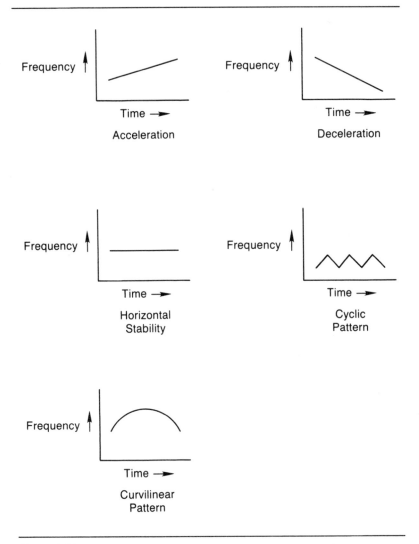

Figure 3.10

graphic trends. In Figures 3.11 and 3.12, even though the same coordinates are employed for graphs A and B, they appear different because the y-axes and x-axes have shrunk or expanded. This elasticity of the axes can lead to distortion and misinterpretation, especially if the coordinates are ignored and only the lines are considered, when examining the graphs.

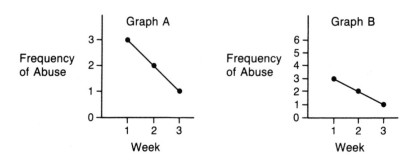

Figure 3.11

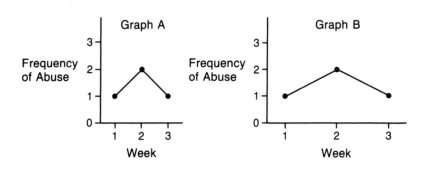

Figure 3.12

Figures 3.13 and 3.14 show how the pictures of graphs can change by mathematical transformations. For the graphs in Figure 3.13, adjacent points in Graph A were averaged (a method for making curves smoother; that is, having fewer fluctuations), resulting in a horizontally stable straight line in Graph B.

The apparent exponential function as represented by original ordinates in Figure 3.14 is changed to an accelerating straight line by taking the square root of each original ordinate and connecting the points.

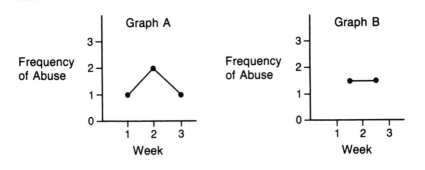

Figure 3.13

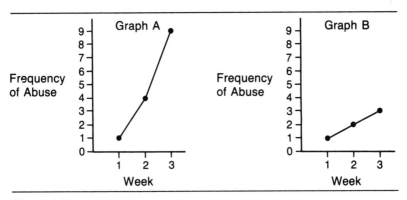

Figure 3.14

USING COMPUTERS TO DRAW GRAPHS

Computer programs are available to perform repetitive and time-consuming graphing of clinical data and to provide support in other areas. Particularly in agencies where microcomputers are accessible and when social workers have the time to become familiar with a program, this approach might be helpful.

There are three general categories of software that can be tapped for this purpose. Software that is primarily intended to be used for graphing, such as Chart, is one option. Another is spreadsheet programs, such as Lotus 1-2-3 or Excel, which often have graphing capabilities as well as the ability to manage data and perform mathematical functions. For

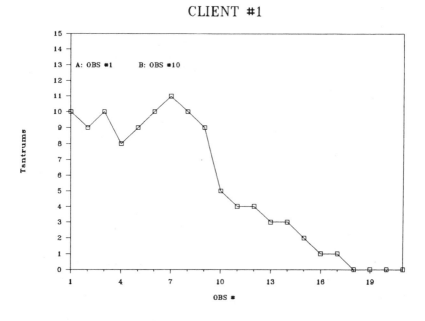

Figure 3.15

example, Lotus 1-2-3 has been programmed to graph client data and to perform some routine statistical tests to analyze the degree of client change (Bronson & Blythe, 1987). Each time additional data are available (perhaps at each weekly session), this information is added to the client's computer file and a new, updated graph can be generated. Figure 3.15 contains a graph (of the frequency of client arguments) drawn by this program.

Another possibility for computer graphing is found in selected computerized assessment tools that also have graphing capabilities. Hudson's Clinical Assessment Package (Hudson, 1982), which is a set of standardized instruments for assessing a range of client problems such as marital and sexual satisfaction, depression, and peer relationships, has been computerized. (Note that Figure 3.2 illustrated the paper-and-pencil version of one of these instruments.) The client can complete the instrument at a computer terminal. The software automatically scores the instrument and, if instructed, will store this score and draw a graph depicting all of the client's scores.

Admittedly, adapting software such as a spreadsheet for a clinical application can be a time-consuming process that may not result in a perfect product. Even when it has been specifically developed for clinical purposes, however, the software may not meet the particular needs of a given agency social worker or client situation. For example, sometimes the time intervals on the x-axis cannot be labeled as clearly or in the exact manner that the worker might want them to be labeled. For workers who enjoy working with computers, these options are attractive. Moreover, new, improved applications are being developed. Nonetheless, a computer is not necessary for graphing data. Social workers can just as well use graph paper to compose their own graphs.

USING BASELINES FOR ASSESSMENT

Constructing Baselines. A baseline is a series of observations about a variable over time, before intervention is instituted. It is typically represented by graphs with at least three time points (Jayaratne & Levy, 1979), although it is much easier to interpret if more than three data points are available. The graphs are constructed as we have previously described in this chapter.

Observations can be gathered for baselines in four basic ways:

1. Making observations during assessment before any intervention takes place.
2. Making observations on a specific problem while intervention is being carried out to address a different problem than the one being baselined.
3. By reconstruction based on archival data and available records.
4. By retrospection based on questionnaires or interviews with clients and/or significant others.

The first method refers to gathering data by any data-gathering device over time before intervention takes place. This requires that there be sufficient time to make observations and that the problem is not so severe that intervention needs to be offered immediately. Ideally, observations should be made until there are clear trends in the graph, indicating that the problem is either accelerating, decelerating, or maintaining the same level of horizontal stability. If observations are made daily, a baseline of 1 to 2 weeks is often feasible. Observations that extend beyond 2 weeks are impractical for most community settings, but might be possible within institutional settings.

The second method of gathering baseline occurs when a worker is making an assessment for a new and/or different problem than that for which the client currently is being treated. Suppose a client is receiving an intervention for relationship difficulties, but is not receiving help for his substance abuse (assuming that the abuse is not so severe as to demand immediate attention). In this instance, a longer baseline could be collected for substance abuse. Further, simultaneously collecting data on substance abuse and the relationship difficulty while only treating the latter problem allows the social worker to examine whether the two problems might be interrelated. In other words, does substance abuse decrease as relationship difficulties diminish? If so, this pattern should show up in information gathered on substance abuse over time.

Reconstructing a baseline is possible if data were already gathered that are relevant to the problem(s) being assessed. Data from the social agency currently serving the client as well as from other social agencies (such as the referring agency) might be available. If so, these data can be graphed and treated as baseline information. Prior to using these data for baselines, however, the social worker should consider whether or not the data are valid. If not, obviously they should not be used.

The least valid data that might be used for baseline are those reconstructed by means of questionnaires and/or interviews. The farther back in time the client seeks to recall events, the greater is the likelihood that there will be distortion of the observations. Attempting to verify reconstructed data by comparing the client's observations with those recalled by significant others is a procedure that might increase the validity of observations. Again, the data should not be used if they are regarded as invalid by the social worker.

Interpreting Baseline Data. Graphs for baselining can be used for assessment to do the following:

1. Determine whether there is a problem.
2. Determine the extent of the problem.
3. Determine whether the problem is persistent.
4. Determine whether intervention should be instituted.

Baselines are graphs about the problem existence, magnitude, duration, and frequency over time. The existence of a problem is determined by operational definitions and the degree to which worker, client, and/or significant others concur about the problem. If there is no problem, intervention may not be necessary. If the problem does not occur as observed by multiple observations over time, the social worker may arrange for periodic observations at future points in time to validate his or her assessment.

Whether or not intervention should be implemented also depends on the severity of the problem as indicated in baselines of problem magnitude, duration, and frequency. The precise definition of a severe degree of problem intensity is derived from clinical judgment based on research and/or experience in working with clients with the particular problem, and on the perceived discomfort of a client. One client may be extremely distraught because he drinks two glasses of wine daily, even though a social worker may believe this is not a serious drinking problem. However, the social worker may gather information about the client's negative attitudes regarding drinking and analyze the strength of those attitudes as well as the drinking behavior, consequently focusing interventions on drinking attitudes and behaviors. In terms of graphic patterns, the social worker should look at the correspondence between problem severity and the numbers representing the ordinates for frequency, duration, and/or magnitude. For example, greater frequency of drinking corresponds with higher ordinate numbers, which are more likely to be associated with problem severity. On the other hand, a graph depicting the number of positive interactions over time represents a different direction related to problem severity. The higher the number of positive interactions (that is, higher ordinate numbers), the less likely is there to be a problem of interactions.

Persistence of problems or lack of problems over time represents a unique advantage of baselines. If the problem dissipates over time through natural resources found in the client or his environment, the worker may shift attention from offering treatment for the problem to considering how the reduced problem status can be maintained and the occurrence of future problems prevented. A graphic pattern of a clinically perceived problem that is high in magnitude, duration, or frequency should be either accelerating or horizontally stable to warrant intervention. A decelerating pattern would lead to the possibility of further observation to determine whether the end result of the downward trend is desirable by worker and client with respect to problem existence or severity. If the rate of deceleration appears to be too slow for worker and client, a goal for intervention might be to increase the rate of deceleration.

The graphic patterns at baseline are used as a benchmark to observe possible changes following the baseline period and associated with the implementation of social work interventions. In addition to visually representing the graphic pattern, it may be helpful to present some simple descriptive statistics that describe average observations for one or more client systems at baseline. The basic statistics employed represent averages of observations at baseline and deviations or dispersions from these average measures. Two measures are the *median* and the *arithmetic mean.* The median is that point in an array of observations at which 50% of the observations are below it and 50% of the observations are above it. If, for example, there are observations regarding the number of times a person makes positive comments and these observations are 10, 12, 14, 15, and 16, the median is 14. If the number of observations is even (for example, 8, 5, 10, and 9), the median is calculated by rank ordering the cases (5, 8, 9, 10), and then taking the arithmetic mean of the two middle cases (8, 9). The arithmetic mean is the sum of the observations divided by the number of observations. Hence, the mean of 8 and 9 is 17 divided by 2, or 8.5, which is the median for the array of 5, 8, 9, and 10. Referring to Figure 3.16, which illustrates a baseline of the number of positive interactions at dinner between a mother and daughter for a period of one week, the median would be derived as follows:

1. Rank order the observations like so (1,1,2,2,2,2,4).
2. Count the number of observations, which is 7.
3. Specify the midpoint of the array of observations, which would be the 4th observation from the bottom (lowest one) and the 4th observation from the top of the array (highest one). The number that corresponds with the midpoint is 2, which is the median.

The mean of that array is calculated as follows: $1 + 2 + 2 + 2 + 2 + 4 + 1/7 = 2$. In this example, the median and the mean coincide, but this is not always the case. The greater the discrepancy between mean and median, the less symmetrical is the array of observations.

Frequently used measures of dispersion are the *range* and the *standard deviation.* The range is simply the highest and lowest cases in a distribution. For Figure 3.16, the range of observations extends from 1 to 4. Thus, data in Figure 3.16 could be described as consisting of 7 observations with a median of 2 and a range extending from 1 to 4 positive interactions. Additionally, the arithmetic mean of 2 and the standard deviation, which is a measure of dispersion, could be indicated.

The standard deviation and its squared value, the *variance,* are statistics that are central to statistical inference with data that are normally distributed (a bell shaped curve comprised of a series of independent, random observations); approximately 99% of the observations are included within 3 standard deviations above and 3 standard

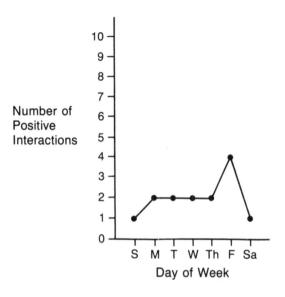

Figure 3.16

deviations below the arithmetic mean. The standard deviation is defined mathematically by formula as the square root of the sum of the squared deviations of observations from their mean $[\Sigma\ (\text{o} - \bar{\text{o}})]^2$ divided by the number of cases less one (N − 1). Turning to Table 3-1 below, the standard deviation is calculated by following these steps:

1. Calculate the arithmetic mean ($\bar{\text{o}}$); this turns out to be 2, as shown in column 1 of Table 3.1.
2. In column 2, the mean is put adjacent to each observation from column 1.
3. Column 3 shows the distance of each observation from the mean.
4. Column 4 indicates the squared value of each entry in column 3. The sum of the values in column 4 or $\Sigma\ (\text{o} - \bar{\text{o}})^2$ is 6; that value divided by N − 1 (7 − 1 = 6) is the variance, which is equal to 6/6 = 1.
5. The square root of 1 equals 1, which is the standard deviation.

To interpret the mean, calculate 2 ± 3 standard deviations [2 + 3 = 5 and 2 − 3 = (−1)]. Theoretically, with a very large number of observations,

Table 3.1 Calculation of a Standard Deviation

Column	1 *Observations* = o	2 $\bar{o}$	3 $(o - \bar{o})$	4 $(o - \bar{o})^2$
	1	2	$1 - 2 = -1$	1
	2	2	$2 - 2 = 0$	0
	2	2	$2 - 2 = 0$	0
	2	2	$2 - 2 = 0$	0
	2	2	$2 - 2 = 0$	0
	4	2	$4 - 2 = 2$	4
	1	2	$1 - 2 = -1$	1
	$14 = \Sigma\, o$			$6 = \Sigma\,(o - \bar{o})^2$

Mean $= \bar{o} = \dfrac{\Sigma\, o}{N} = \dfrac{14}{7} = 2$

Variance $= \dfrac{\Sigma\,(o - \bar{o})^2}{N - 1} = \dfrac{6}{6} = 1$

Standard Deviation $= \sqrt{1} = 1$

99% of them would lie between 5 and 0 (since −1 is meaningless for this example).

For Figure 3.16, median and range would be sufficient for describing the distribution. The mean and the standard deviation are more appropriate for describing distributions with more observations, and for comparing the observations at intervention with those at baseline. For a more detailed exposition of descriptive statistics, the reader can refer to any standard textbook in statistics, such as Hays's (1973) *Statistics for the Social Sciences.*

USING NORMATIVE DATA FOR ASSESSMENT

Normative data are data that are averaged (mean or median) and presented typically with ranges and/or standard deviations. The data are based on observations of many persons who may be representative of some particular population(s). Normative data rarely include observations over more than two points in time. These data are often available for psychological tests and may be for variables derived from other data-gathering procedures such as questionnaires.

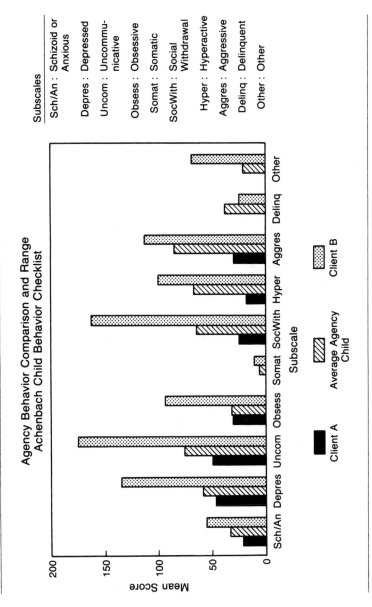

Figure 3.17

Normative data can be used for assessment purposes to compare measurements of one client with those of a representative population whose characteristics are known. For example, a social worker may observe the extent to which a child's reading score is below, the same, or higher than the average of other children of his age, gender, and grade. A pictorial way to make such comparisons is to draw a bar graph comparing clients to an average group of clients. For example, in Figure 3.17, the scores on the Achenbach Child Behavior Check List for client B are compared with those of the average village child (mean scores for children in this residential treatment center) and a child who is regarded as relatively well-adjusted, client A.

Caution must be exerted in using normative data with specific clients. To begin, estimate whether the normative data are representative of a population against which the specific client should be compared. Secondly, make a judgment regarding the reliability and validity of the normative data. Third, determine if there are any data regarding averages and dispersions (such as standard deviations), and whether there are any validating data that have predictive or concurrent validity. If these conditions are met, the location of a client as typical or not typical of a particular population (such as apparently psychologically adjusted teenagers, public assistance recipients, chronic schizophrenics, or unemployed fathers) can have implications for the type of interventions one might plan. Referring to Figure 3.17, it is obvious that on all subscales of Achenbach's list of child behavior problems, with the exception of delinquency, client B exhibits more problematic behavior than that of the average child in residential treatment. This may mean that he needs more special attention and may be less likely to respond to the routine interventions given in residential treatment.

EXERCISES

1. (a) Select two instruments that can yield Type 1 and/or Type 3 data. Discuss the extent to which they are or are not useful for assessing clients in an agency with which you are familiar.
   (b) Discuss the potential errors and biases you might encounter when using those instruments in an agency. Consider how you might overcome these.
2. Define and give examples of problem existence, problem magnitude, problem duration, and problem frequency as they pertain to one or more clients with whom you work(ed).

3. (a) Make observations for 1-2 weeks for one of your clients on one variable related to assessment. Plot a graph, and calculate the mean, median, range, and standard deviation for the data you collected.

    (b) Describe the trends you observe in the graph.

Chapter 4

PLANNING INTERVENTIONS

Having determined the problem confronting a client, the social worker uses the assessment information to plan the interventions believed to be most suitable for dealing with client problems. In this planning process, there are four basic steps which should take place: selecting problems for intervention, specifying intervention objectives, choosing interventions, and describing interventions that the social worker intends to use to accomplish the intervention objectives. A knowledge of measurement concepts and principles can help the social worker in making key decisions that facilitate the accomplishment of each of these steps.

SELECTING PROBLEMS FOR INTERVENTION

As a result of an assessment, the social worker typically uncovers a set of multiple problems and needs and must identify which problems will be worked on and in what order. Although the principal function of an agency may be to deal with a single problem, such as substance abuse in an industrial setting, there are usually other related problems experienced by each individual client or client system. Related to substance abuse may be problems in interpersonal relationships, criminal activities for obtaining money for drugs, or isolation from friends. Obviously, the worker refers to other resources when necessary, depending on the type of agency in which the worker is employed and the worker's skills. Sometimes there is only one problem that needs to be addressed. In these rare instances, there is no need to select problems for intervention.

PROBLEM HIERARCHY

One way to choose among several problems that may require interventions is to construct a problem hierarchy, which is a list of those problems, arranged in order of priority, that the worker or worker and client believe need resolution. Problems of lower priority may be put aside or not even worked on, while at higher levels of priority, two or more problems may be addressed simultaneously or sequentially.

To construct a problem hierarchy, the list of problems (typically unordered by priority) indicated from assessment is studied. For each of these problems, there should be basic information that pertains to a problem's existence, magnitude, duration, and/or frequency, as described in the previous chapter. Second, the need to remove problems from the list is considered. This is accomplished by eliminating those problems that have a very low degree of magnitude or are in the process of resolution without any intervention. For example, baseline data may indicate that an adolescent's tardiness to class has been sufficiently reduced so that it is comparable to the average student's tardiness, and it may not be perceived as a problem by the youth, his parents, and the school. The magnitude or intensity of a problem may not have achieved a high enough score on an instrument to suggest it is a clinical problem; hence that problem might also be eliminated from the list.

The determination of the order in which problems should be addressed is based on the worker's judgment and experience, as well as the agency and environmental resources that can be enlisted. Agency purposes and function put certain constraints on how well a worker can deal with a problem. For example, a client's basic set of problems may be related to a medical regimen he needs to follow. Social factors related to the client's illness may be more appropriately addressed in a medical setting than in a social agency that has no relationship to the client's hospitalization and outpatient services. A disabled client may primarily need employment, which may be more appropriate to discuss at a vocational rehabilitation center rather than at a family service agency. Hence, problems that are directly dealt with at the agency may be regarded as a different order from those that need to be referred to other agencies. If prospective clients can only receive help by being referred to other agencies, they should be referred.

A fundamental task in constructing a problem hierarchy is to consider whether any of the problems are life threatening or dangerous. Potential suicide, violent behavior, and psychotic episodes are examples of problems that require immediate action and would be placed at the top of a problem hierarchy.

A fourth consideration is that of the client's volition regarding problem resolution. The worker needs to consider the client's desires in relation to the problems. Does the client feel uncomfortable about and desire to reduce or eliminate some problems? Sometimes a social worker may choose to first address a problem that is important to the client, although it seems less urgent to the worker, as a way of engaging the client in the treatment process. For example, a client may have experienced a series of personal crises that have exacerbated his feeling of low-esteem and lack of confidence. The problem with the highest priority may have to do with whether or not he will act to dissolve his marriage. Yet, the social worker may first want to intervene at a smaller scale to help the client achieve a task that will increase his self-confidence, such as helping a local drama club that is in need of accounting skills he or she possesses.

Fifth, the worker might consider whether change in some other condition is necessary before a client's problem(s) can be ameliorated. If so, the condition may be regarded as an important problem that needs immediate attention. For example, a single parent who is receiving AFDC benefits may desire to manage her children better, and the social worker may believe the client is in need of parenting skills to reduce her children's aggressive behavior and disobedience. A more basic need, however, may have to be met first, such as helping the client clean the house and turn on the heat (in winter) before assisting her in parenting. In this case, the demands for a clean house and adequate heating take priority over the need to increase parenting skills.

Finally, within the constraints of the agency in which the worker is employed as well as the previous considerations discussed above, priorities are determined in part by the social worker's theoretical and practical orientation to practice. Some workers believe there should be contractual agreements made between client(s) and worker; others believe that there are many instances when contracts are not possible or not necessary to pursue. Obviously, contractual agreements would require that worker and client agree on the problem hierarchy. This is accomplished by worker and client reviewing the list and then negotiating those problems that will be regarded as most important and on which interventions will be focused.

There are many instances where it is required by law that certain behaviors be reported and that interventions be provided to reduce these problem behaviors — child abuse, spouse abuse, criminal activities, and drug use at work and school are examples. Many clients exhibiting such behaviors are mandated to receive help, but they may not be willing to engage in negotiating a treatment contract.

Furthermore, the theoretical orientation of some workers may indicate that the clients do not have adequate expertise to diagnose and assess problems. Although client input is sought to increase the worker's understanding, the worker alone develops the problem hierarchy because her or his theoretical orientation dictates that it is the worker's responsibility to make decisions regarding problem importance, based on his or her expertise. The worker then attempts to involve the client(s) in the intervention process, however, seeking to engage the client in treatment and increase the client's motivation.

A treatment hierarchy may contain 5-10 problems, depending on the case and the extent of the initial assessment. Some problems will be apparently related; some will seem disparate, perhaps requiring different interventions. A social worker may work on two or more problems at a time if they are related or if it makes clinical sense to do so. For example, a worker may work with a family with a predelinquent adolescent involved in disruptive activities at home as well as at school. The worker may simultaneously work with the parents and the adolescent to reduce the adolescent's disruptive activities at home and school, since these are related activities. If the adolescent is also interested in losing weight (and if this had not been a source of family or school tension) to increase his athletic performance, the problem of weight may be seen as less related. But the worker might elect to work on this problem if it seems important to the adolescent. Doing so might help enhance the worker's relationship with the adolescent, which in turn might facilitate the accomplishment of family goals.

Of course, there must be sufficient time for the social worker to work with the client. Some problems may lead to interventions that require more time than others. Obviously, if a voluntary client desires immediate change and it is not possible, that client may simply withdraw from treatment. Some estimation by the worker on how long it will take to resolve problems can assist in the development of a problem hierarchy. Even if resolved, some problems are not of a short-term nature and may require vigilant maintenance and follow-up procedures. Chronic illness, alcoholism, and drug abuse are examples.

SPECIFYING INTERVENTION OBJECTIVES
AND HYPOTHESES

The process of specifying intervention objectives can assist the social worker in making decisions about which problems to work on from a problem hierarchy. Specifying intervention objectives helps to determine if there is overlap in the objectives themselves or in the expected timing of their resolution.

Since the purpose of deploying interventions is to reduce problems or prevent their occurrence, specifying objectives involves identifying the expected change or lack of change in relation to problem existence, magnitude, duration, and/or frequency. For example, an intervention objective for a family might be that the members of the family increase the amount of time they spend together in recreational activities. An objective for a marital couple might be preventing the dissolution of their marriage.

Objectives about Prevention. If the objective is focused on prevention, it can be specified by indicating the problem that is to be prevented from occurring, as in the previous example of preventing the breakup of a marriage. To make the objective even more specific, the time frame during which the problem is expected to not occur (that is, be prevented) can be identified. If, as an example, a group of adolescent girls are receiving a group intervention to prevent pregnancy, the objective might be to prevent unplanned pregnancies among the group members for a period of three years following the completion of the group.

Objectives about Change. Change objectives are those that refer to problem resolution by reducing the magnitude or frequency of the problem and/or its duration, or by completely eliminating the problem so that it no longer exists. For instance, for a client who experiences a fear of being alone, a social worker might have an objective to eradicate the fear, reduce the strength or intensity of the fear, reduce the number of times the fear occurs, or reduce the length of time the client is anxious or fearful when left alone.

By operationalizing the measurement of the problem, the objectives are linked to the treatment process. This enables the worker to be more precise in measuring the extent to which the objective is accomplished. Referring to Chapter 2, the reader can observe that this further specification includes an indication of the types of data that are to be gathered. For example, one objective for a couple seeking marital counseling might be for the couple to increase their reported satisfaction on a standardized marital satisfaction instrument. Note that the reduction of the problem might occur with either an increase or decrease in variables related to the problem. In this instance, the problem might have been lack of satisfaction in the marriage, and an increase in marital satisfaction would indicate a decrease in the marital problem.

There may be more than one objective that is expected to be the result of an intervention or set of interventions. A couple experiencing relationship problems may have the following objectives: increase their reported marital satisfaction, reduce the frequency of negative comments made to one another, and increase the frequency of sexual intercourse. The social worker may use the same intervention or set of interventions to attain all of the objectives or may have individual interventive plans for each objective. As much as possible, each objective should be tied to a specific intervention or set of interventions, so that the social worker can accumulate and develop knowledge regarding interventions that are more or less effective in addressing specific client problems. Determining what intervention(s) brought about specific changes, however, is seen as less important than simply knowing, with the support of some form of measurement, that change in the desired direction occurred.

A way to specify an intervention objective further is to indicate, if appropriate, (1) the amount of change expected in terms of problem magnitude or frequency; (2) when that change is expected to occur; and/or (3) for how long it is expected that the change will endure. For example, it might be expected as a result of intervention that a client might make more positive than negative comments to his spouse within one month after the onset of intervention, and that the greater amount of positive comments will persist in the couples' interactions for at least six months after intervention.

Instrumental vs. Final Objectives. An instrumental objective is an objective that, if accomplished, permits the attainment of a more remote objective (Nelsen, 1983). It is a necessary condition that must be fulfilled before a final objective can be realized. For example, a child might need to control her aggression before she can play cooperatively with her peers. The control of aggression is an objective that is instrumental to accomplishing the final objective of playing cooperatively with her peers.

Instrumental objectives are more immediate in time than are final objectives. They serve to reduce long-range objectives to more manageable proportions for the social worker and the client. Some long-range objectives, such as the development of an active social life, might be extremely difficult for a reclusive older client; yet accomplishing smaller, tangible goals, such as calling a neighbor once a week and getting information about activities for senior citizens, would be indicative of progress. As another example, a delinquent boy may still engage in delinquent activity, but his behavior may not be harmful to others and he may have improved his performance at school somewhat and strengthened his relationship with his family. Although the increments are smaller, these goals may be more attainable and, therefore, offer more encouragement to the client (and the worker). The task of the worker is to identify realistic goals that are achievable and beneficial for clients, yet are not so trivial that they are of little consequence.

Intervention Hypotheses. An intervention hypothesis is a statement of a predicted relationship between an intervention and an expected consequence, or objective, of that intervention. The intervention is an independent variable that is antecedent to and presumably causally related to one or more dependent variables, which are intervention objectives. Thus, planning an intervention is essentially the formation of a treatment hypothesis that specifies independent and dependent variables.

There are two basic types of intervention hypotheses. One type relates the intervention to an objective that may be immediate or remote and may or may not be instrumental. For example, a paradoxical intervention may have the objective of changing an adolescent girl's behavior so that she keeps her bedroom neat and clean, which may be an important change in itself, or may be instrumental in subsequently changing her relationship with her mother, who detests a sloppy house.

A second type of intervention hypothesis is one which states a relationship between an independent variable, an intervening variable, and a dependent variable. An intervening variable is a variable that is causally connected with, and occurs in time between, an independent and dependent variable. First, it is predicted that the intervening variable will change as a result of intervention, the independent variable. Then, the hypothesis predicts that the dependent variable will be affected by the change in the intervening variable. For example, a social worker might be working with an individual who has headaches that are not apparently due to physiological, chemical, or physical variables. As a part of assessment, the client may have graphed the occurrence of the headaches over a 2-week period. Whenever the client had a headache, he was asked to write down possible antecedent conditions. The worker might have observed that the client indicated he felt angry toward a family member just before he had headaches. Exploration in an interview with these data may lead the worker to hypothesize that headaches would be reduced if the client expresses his anger. Therefore, the worker plans an intervention to increase the client's direct expression of anger. As the client expresses anger (the intervening variable), it is predicted that the frequency of headaches will decrease.

Forming Intervention Hypotheses. To form intervention hypotheses, a worker must do the following:

1. Indicate whether treatment objectives are to deal with prevention, maintenance, or change.

2. Operationalize objectives in terms of problem existence, magnitude, frequency, and/or duration, specifying the type of data needed to measure variable(s) related to the objective. This process is specification of the dependent variable.

3. Based on the assessment, consider whether there are any intervening variables that can affect the dependent variables.

4. State predictions about the interventions, or independent variables. These predictions may take the form of independent variable X leads to dependent variable Y, or independent variable X affects intervening variable Y, which in turn affects dependent variable Z.

CHOOSING INTERVENTIONS

Interventions are actions that social workers take with client systems to achieve specified objectives. They are employed to reduce, eliminate, or prevent problems. Interventions may be complex, involving a set of behaviors, attitudes, and beliefs that prescribe, or simply suggest, worker interactions with clients, or they may be relatively simple and specific. Interventions may be a well-established set of actions originating in a particular theory or model of practice or they may be practice innovations that are newly developed in response to client needs. Often, suggestions for possible interventions originate in supervisory conferences or in formal or informal discussions with colleagues. Part of the planning process in social work practice with individuals, groups, and families involves the possible selection of available interventions. The following criteria should be considered when choosing an intervention: relevance, worker fit, client fit, empirical support, specificity, and cost.

The intervention should be relevant to the problem situation of the client. If the intervention, for example, is designed for long-term treatment and the client's problem demands a brief, intensive treatment, the intervention is irrelevant for that specific problem. An intervention based on specific dyadic interactions between a marital couple obviously is irrelevant for work with only one spouse.

Worker fit and client fit are similar to the notion of relevance. Worker fit refers to the extent to which the intervention is compatible with the worker's style, values, skills, and ability. The worker should be comfortable using the intervention, and it should fit with his or her values and assumptions regarding interventions for particular clients. Correspondingly, the intervention should fit with the client's style, values, skills, or abilities. If, for example, a client has few verbal skills, cognitive intervention might be inappropriate.

The extent to which the worker and/or client lack certain abilities, skills, or knowledge to implement particular interventions needs to be examined. Considerable training in group process may be necessary before a given worker can lead a task-oriented group. Or, clients may be unavailable to implement behavioral reinforcement schedules at home if the intervention requires strong motivation or skill in observation. On the other hand, interventions that require client participation, such as reinforcement schedules, may be able to incorporate training in the use of the intervention and the decision to select the intervention may depend on having sufficient time and resources to cover the extra training needed. Often, during the assessment phase, the worker can determine if the client will benefit from a particular intervention or if training or adaptation of the intervention will be needed, and can be carried out without too much expenditure of resources.

To the extent possible, interventions should have some experiential and/or empirical support. If the intervention was used successfully by other practitioners, a worker is more likely to choose it for his or her own work. Empirical support refers to the use of data for verifying relationships between interventions and dependent variables. Obviously, the empirical support should be examined to determine if it is sound and if it applies to the current client or client system. The variables in the study or studies in question should be reliable. They should be generalizable to other situations, particularly the ones being addressed with the client at hand. Evidence for effectiveness should show that there is an association between the intervention and the dependent variables. Further, the measurement of the independent and dependent variables should be reliable and valid, and variables other than the intervention should not be responsible for the association. There also should be supportive evidence that the intervention is *effective,* that is, related to the attainment of the interventive objectives. When equally effective interventions are compared, *efficiency* is an important criterion of selection. Efficiency is the ratio of effectiveness to the cost of the intervention, as determined by time and money. Equal effectiveness at lower costs is preferable, other things being equal

(Tripodi & Epstein, 1980, pp. 79-84). For example, a possible intervention for an abusive mother may be an intensive, short-term treatment program that helps her get her house cleaned, uses rational-emotive therapy to help her control her anger, and behavioral skills training to teach her effective, nonphysical methods of disciplining her children. Another intervention might involve attending 12 weekly sessions of a parenting group coupled with individual psychotherapy to help her understand conflicted feelings about parenting. If the effectiveness of both intervention plans appeared to be equal, the former plan would be more desirable if it is cheaper in terms of time and money, thereby yielding a higher efficiency score. Conversely, if the latter intervention plan had greater effectiveness, this might offset the more favorable length and cost of treatment for the first plan, making the psychotherapy and parenting group the more efficient intervention. Evidence for effectiveness should show that there is an association between the intervention and the dependent variables; the measurement of intervention and the dependent variables should be reliable and valid, and variables other than the intervention should not be responsible for the association (Tripodi & Epstein, 1980). Unfortunately, precise information about the effectiveness and even the cost or length of interventions often is unavailable, so workers must estimate these factors.

A social worker cannot adopt an intervention unless she or he knows specifically what is involved in carrying out the intervention. As they become more specific and detailed, interventions are more likely to be adopted. To implement a new intervention, a social worker may require training, role play simulations, and instructional materials. The social worker should review these materials and other descriptive information to see if it is sufficiently detailed and to determine if the intervention is compatible with her or his theoretical orientation to practice.

Costs for using an intervention are determined by such things as the time it takes to implement the intervention, the amount and type of equipment needed (such as forms, computer, telephone, or tape recorder), the number of people involved, and the location of the intervention.

To some extent, the choice of interventions is constrained by the agency in which the social worker is employed. Agency resources, complexity, staff, and caseload influence choices of specific interventions. Such parameters as location of interviews (in the worker's office versus in the client's home, for example), time of appointments, other geographic considerations, available equipment, theoretical orientation of the agency, and populations with which the agency deals are influential. Although workers are more likely to select interventions that are consistent with their own theoretical orientations, there may be some interventions that represent different orientations but are more pragmatic in terms of such factors as cost. Social workers should carefully review the potential of such interventions, especially if they are supported by considerable empirical evidence.

DESCRIBING INTERVENTIONS

It is impossible to describe every action and utterance necessary for a social worker to accomplish intervention objectives. Unplanned circumstances affect the degree and timing of implementing interventions. For example, the worker or client may miss appointments, be sick, or have a crisis situation to handle. Interactions between people cannot be completely programmed because all contingencies cannot be anticipated. Yet there needs to be some amount of specificity and communality in approaches for certain types of problems if we seek to train others in the use of methods, to test our interventions, and to develop knowledge about when specific interventions are most useful. Moreover, if we wish to change interventions when they do not appear to be working for a particular client system, we need to know what it is that we should change; without a minimum amount of specificity, the task would be hopeless. A worker can indicate certain parameters that remain relatively stable across interventions and can delineate content areas that are planned to be covered with a relative degree of specificity. Relatively stable parameters include appointment dates, time length of intervention sessions, number of interventions, when and where the interventions should be delivered, who delivers the intervention, and the target(s) of the intervention (such as individual client, family, or group). Content areas refer to such things as topics of discussion, nature of tasks, and types of worker involvement. The social worker's theoretical orientation should be indicated in the planned intervention, for it includes assumptions about clients' attitudes and behaviors and presumes certain ways in which the workers will operate. Theoretical orientation is not enough, however, because its application varies from worker to worker, and often workers have different understandings and methods of operating, even when they indicate that they subscribe to the same theoretical orientation. Hence, the mere statement of psychoanalytic, cognitive, behavioral, ecological, or other approaches is not sufficiently specific. The social worker is more specific when necessary actions and attitudes are indicated. Examples of more specific descriptions are: the use of supportive phrases to develop an initial client-worker relationship; the use of praise when a client is able to analyze his recent behavior as a manifestation of past occurrences; and role playing a stressful situation and discussing the feelings that were or might be encountered in a real situation. Obviously, these descriptions can be made even more specific. Essentially, the social worker indicates what interactions with the client system are planned.

Group interventions frequently are described in some detail. Co-leaders may want to ensure that they can work together smoothly and help the group accomplish its goals by following outlines or scripts describing the intervention components. Or, group leaders may want to have certain content presented, discussed, and/or experienced by group members, while also allowing time for group members to introduce some subjects for discussion. As an example, Berlin (1985) identifies the components of the relapse prevention treatment for a group of women trying to reduce self-criticism. Each component is described, and topics to discuss or exercises or tasks to ask the women to perform are presented.

There are several useful concepts that help in describing interventions sufficiently to allow them to be used again by the workers themselves, as well as their colleagues and students. These concepts are procedural descriptiveness, specifying involvement, determining settings for interventions, and developing practice prescriptions.

Procedural Descriptiveness. Thomas and his colleagues have argued that the objectives of social work practice are accomplished mainly by procedures. Interventions are ". . . guided and otherwise mediated by the procedures that helping agents and others are to follow in providing . . ." services (Thomas, Bastien, Stuebe, Bronson, & Yaffe, 1987, p. 44). The concept of procedural descriptiveness essentially states that a procedure is described to the extent that the description is specific and complete. In terms of practice, *specific* and *complete* are defined as:

". . . for a procedure to be complete, it should indicate (a) the behaviors that are to be carried out in order to accomplish a given objective, (b) the person(s) who should engage in the behaviors, (c) the target person(s), or clientele who are to be affected by the procedure, (d) the conditions under which the behaviors are to be carried out, and (e) the goals that will be accomplished through the use of the procedure. To be specific, a procedure should denote the precise details of the activities to be performed. The description should be clear in that it is readable and unambiguous for the user, and it should refer to the observable characteristics of the activities to be performed . . ." (Thomas, et al., 1987, p. 45).

An example is provided by Gambrill, Thomas, and Carter (1971), who attempt to delineate procedural guidelines for social workers with a sociobehavioral orientation. They divided social worker's activities into 12 procedural steps, which are intended to guide worker behaviors in open settings. Although they can become much more specific as they can be related to a particular worker and client with a specific set of problems, these steps, nonetheless, illustrate content areas that can be specified in an intervention process. They further indicate how workers can specify procedures in their interactions with clients within each of the content areas. The objectives for each of the 12 steps are:

1. "To obtain the spectrum of presenting problems as seen by the client and the worker." (p. 52)

2. "To reach a verbal or written agreement with the client concerning which one of the problem areas needs the most immediate attention." (p. 52)

3. "To obtain the client's agreement to cooperate fully in the activities associated with assessment and modification." (p. 53)

4. "To denote specific behaviors of the client and relevant others associated with him that constitute the essential elements of the selected problem area." (p. 53)

5. "To obtain a preintervention estimate of the frequency, magnitude, or duration of the specified problem behaviors." (p. 54)

6. "To isolate the stimuli that precede and follow the problem behavior and serve to control its occurrence." (pp. 54-55)

7. "To determine what environmental resources may be used in the modification of behavior." (p. 55)

8. "To specify the behavioral objectives of the modification plan." (p. 56)

9. "To select an appropriate behavioral modification role for the worker and the modification techniques to use in achieving the behavioral objectives." (p. 56)

10. "To modify or maintain behavior with respect to the modification objectives and the contract made with the client." (p. 58)

11. "To obtain information concerning the effectiveness of intervention." (p. 69)

12. "To achieve the maintenance and stabilization of the desired terminal behaviors for which intervention was undertaken." (p. 60) (Gambrill, Thomas, & Carter, 1971, pp. 52-60)

Specifying Involvement. The specification of involvement in intervention refers to the nature and extent of participation by key actors in the provision of intervention. The key actors typically are the social worker and the client system. In some situations, critical people also may include other professionals in a treatment team, paraprofessionals, peers, or social workers at other agencies. For example, a family may be receiving services or otherwise have contact with the local public assistance office, child protective services, a correctional facility, and a mental health agency.

When clients receive services from more than one social agency, the planning of an intervention must include efforts to coordinate the activities of the various human service providers. If such coordination does not occur, an intervention planned in one agency might be at cross-purposes with other interventions planned by other agencies. For example, a worker in a mental health agency may not try to uncover a client's defenses on the basis that this could lead to a recurrence of the client's psychotic behaviors. In opposition, a worker in a public assistance office might assume that more understanding of a client's own contribution to his problems will help him change his behavior and ultimately secure a steady job. Hence, this worker might make more probing than supportive statements in interviews with the client, and inadvertently uncover the client's defenses.

There may be significant others who also are involved with the social worker's intervention. A child might be the target of an intervention. His parents might also be part of the client system or they might serve as part of the intervention, working closely with the worker, to systematically employ an aspect of the intervention at home (such as consistency of rewards, observations of particular behaviors, or assisting the child in tasks related to the intervention). Other significant persons might also be involved with other clients, such as relatives, friends, and employers.

The extent of involvement could also be specified. How often are the key actors involved in intervention? Do they attend all interventive sessions? How much time is spent in each contact, or on tasks that relate to the client's intervention?

Determining Settings for Interventions. The effectiveness and efficiency of interventions can vary in relation to where the intervention is implemented. Some settings may be more or less accessible to clients depending on such things as the distance between the agency and the clients' homes, availability of transportation to the intervention site, and specific eligibility requirements. In fact, some interventions may be designed principally for the purpose of increasing client access to the receipt of service.

Intervention sites can be formal or informal. Formal sites are social agencies and other organizations that provide human services such as churches and police stations, while examples of informal sites are clients' homes or fast food restaurants.

The intervention site should be specified as part of the intervention process. It should be determined in relation to whether it facilitates the implementation of the intervention plan and the accomplishment of intervention objectives. It should be a place that is affordable and accessible to the client. As much as possible, the site should maintain a client's privacy and other rights, as well as have sufficient resources for carrying out interventions. Obviously, with some clients the number of possible intervention sites is limited. A client confined to bed in a nursing home, for instance, will have to receive intervention in the nursing home, although it would be possible to experiment with delivering the intervention over the telephone if agency resources precluded regular travel to the nursing home.

Developing Practice Prescriptions. Another way to specify and describe more completely an intervention is to develop practice prescriptions (or proscriptions) and consider the extent to which they can be generalized (Wedenoja, Nurius, & Tripodi, 1988). Practice prescriptions are defined as ". . . statements which instruct practitioners in what to do, be, think, or say when working with clients or on behalf of clients" (Wedenoja et al., p. 429). Practice prescriptions are often of a form indicating that the social worker should, must, needs to, or has to think, feel, or engage in an action in certain prescribed ways. To illustrate, a prescription might be as follows: When a social worker develops a group focusing on guided group interactions for delinquent boys, individual contracts must be negotiated with each boy regarding personal goals (Wedenoja et al., 1988).

Prescriptions can be constructed by referring to questions or guidelines such as these:

1. For what type of client and practice setting is this prescription designed? What client characteristics, such as gender, ethnicity, previous treatment history, or cognitive abilities, are particularly relevant?

2. What intervention or specific interventive technique should the social worker implement? Is the intervention sufficiently described so that it could be replicated by the same or another worker?

3. What is the rationale for selecting this prescription? What empirical or other evidence is there for using this prescription?

4. With what types of clients, presenting problems, specific treatment objectives, agency settings, and social workers is the prescription known or not known to be effective or appropriate? What modifications might be necessary because of these concerns?

5. How might this be applied in other situations?

(Adapted from Wedenoja, Nurius, & Tripodi, 1988).

Practice prescriptions vary in their degree of abstractness and in the amount of detail that is specified. But they also differ in relation to the strength of the empirical base. Prescriptions can be evaluated by employing concepts from measurement to appraise the extent to which the prescription is or is not empirically based. Wedenoja and her colleagues (1988) suggest that representativeness, replication, supporting evidence, reference to limitations, and reference to further generalization should be considered. *Representativeness* is the extent to which the prescription has been derived from experience with and research on clients that are representative of the client population. A practice prescription based on intervention with delinquent females is not representative and necessarily generalizable to nondelinquent males, for example. *Replication* is the repetition of an intervention by different social workers, in different settings, and different clients, with consistent results suggesting effectiveness. The more replications, the more generalizable is the practice prescription. *Supporting evidence* refers to the actual research and/or practice experiences that justify the practice prescription. Obviously, a prescription should not dictate how to act, think, or feel if these attitudes and behaviors are not related to effectiveness. *Reference to limitations* refers to the extent to which practice prescriptions are limited in terms of generalizability, while *reference to further generalization* indicates that the prescriber believes the prescription can be generalized to other populations in spite of the fact that there is no available supporting evidence to justify that assertion of generality.

Basically, prescriptions can be focused on specific types of client populations and the worker's roles and behaviors in delivering interventions can be described in some detail. These prescriptions should be offered under one of two conditions. First, there is supporting evidence that justifies the prescriptions's practice effectiveness, relevance, and generalizability. Or, the prescription is offered as an hypothesis that will be tested in the clinical situation. In this case, it is not assumed that the intervention contained within the prescription is effective or generalizable in practice. This second condition is the one most likely to prevail in much of our work with clients, which heightens the need to determine how a planned intervention is implemented and whether it will be effective for particular clients.

EXERCISES

1. Construct problem hierarchies for two clients. Discuss what factors are similar or different in influencing your ordering of intervention priorities for those clients.

2. Specify change objectives, instrumental and final, for one of your clients.

3. Develop an intervention hypothesis, relating an instrumental objective to a final objective.

4. Describe interventions you use for two different clients. To what extent is it possible for a colleague to deliver an intervention similar to the ones you described? Are they sufficiently descriptive and complete?

5. Develop a practice prescription that you believe is grounded in practice experience or based on research findings. Evaluate the prescription in terms of the evidence for practice effectiveness and generalizability.

Chapter 5

IMPLEMENTING INTERVENTIONS

Even the best plans by the best social worker can go awry. The experienced social worker observes the degree to which the intervention plans are actually applicable as the case progresses. If there is an implementation failure, the intervention is altered or modified, if at all possible in the particular practice situation. The purpose of this chapter is to employ measurement concepts and principles to facilitate the implementation of social work interventions. First, we shall introduce methods for considering the reliability and validity of the intervention procedures. Second, possible implementation problems will be described and ways to correct for them will be discussed briefly. The purpose here is to indicate to social workers what kinds of potential problems they should scan for, when monitoring or observing the intervention procedures. Third, several ways of assessing client progress after interventions are implemented will be considered.

INTERVENTION RELIABILITY AND VALIDITY

Two basic concepts in research on behavioral analysis are useful to describe intervention reliability and validity: treatment integrity (Peterson, Homer, & Wonderlich, 1982; Salend, 1984) and procedural reliability (Billingsley, White, & Munson, 1980). *Treatment integrity* refers to the degree to which a treatment or intervention is implemented as it was planned. This essentially is analogous to the validity or accuracy of the implementation. Correspondingly, *procedural reliability* is the degree to which procedures or interventions are consistently implemented from time to time and across different workers.

A problem confronting both intervention researchers and practitioners is that of variability in implementation. Intervention can be standardized only to the degree to which variability can be reduced. Variability can occur as a result of inconsistency in application of intervention procedures as well as a number of unforeseen factors such as environmental stresses and unplanned contingencies. But why is it necessary to try to standardize interventions given the multiplicity of factors that may interact differently from client to client?

Standardization of intervention, to the degree it is possible, allows us to know what we did in our efforts to help a particular client. This enables us to be accountable to the client and ourselves in describing what took place. This is important, regardless of intervention success. If intervention objectives are not accomplished, it is important for the social worker to know exactly what intervention was delivered so that it can be ceased or modified. If, on the other hand, the intervention was successful, it is then necessary to describe it so it can be taught to students, tried by colleagues, used by the social worker with the same or other clients, and evaluated systematically to contribute to the profession.

Obviously, it is important to accurately and consistently implement a planned intervention. To begin, simply knowing that variability in implementation procedures is possible can help a social worker look for ways to reduce that variability. In fact, it is the unawareness of variability in implementation that has previously led to some of the problems in interpreting results in psychotherapy outcome research. This is simply a restatement of the problem noted by many practitioners that one cannot evaluate a practice within a particular research study if the practice or intervention itself, that is the independent variable in intervention hypotheses, is not standardized. This problem of variability in applying an intervention is a phenomenon referred to as *treatment drift* by Peterson et al. (1982) and *treatment shift* by McMahon (1987). Whereas treatment drift is a phenomenon in which a treatment agent (such as a social worker) does not adhere to a regimen prescribed by an experimenter in intervention research, treatment shift is identified more broadly and occurs "when a social worker knowingly or unknowingly deviates from an established procedure" (McMahon, 1987, p. 13).

An example of worker unreliability in the implementation of treatment is as follows. Suppose a social worker is attempting to strengthen the self-concept of an adolescent male. The intervention involves only the use of positive comments in reference to the boy's behaviors, said in a pleasant, relatively objective manner by the worker. The intervention is implemented inconsistently if these events occur:

1. The worker forgets the plan and emits no or varying properties of positive statements in relation to negative statements.
2. Positive statements are made, but sometimes mechanically with no felt enthusiasm and animatedly at other times.
3. The worker's anger, fatigue, or other events penetrate his or her actions. In this instance, the worker's apparent moods are perceived as displeasure with the client, regardless of whether the verbal content is positive.
4. The boy is involved in delinquent activity which the worker strongly opposes, consequently berating the boy, and deviating or shifting from the intended intervention plan.

It is possible for an intervention to shift not because of the worker, but because of the involvement of the client system in intervention. Suppose that an intervention involves the mother of the teen-aged boy. The mother is supposed to ask her son if he has completed his homework each night, and to praise him if he has done so. She may do that task inconsistently. The social worker, assuming the mother consistently applied the task, would not be aware of that source of intervention unreliability.

MONITORING INTERVENTION IMPLEMENTATION

Monitoring is a systematic observation of the degree to which an intervention is consistently implemented as intended. It involves a planned system of observation to enhance the reliability and validity of the implementation of the intervention.

To monitor interventions, it is necessary to know the ingredients and parameters of the intervention so that procedures for observing whether the intervention is implemented can be specified. Monitoring may identify possible reasons for implementation failure when it occurs so that corrective remedies can be considered.

In developing intervention plans, as described more fully in Chapter 4, the social worker attempts to specify the interventions. Who does what? How often and for what duration? What contents are to be covered? What content areas should be ignored? Does the intervention call for specific worker attributes, such as race, gender, or life experience? Answers to questions like these give a range of possible phenomena to consider.

				Days of Week			
	Sun.	Mon.	Tues.	Wed.	Thurs.	Fri.	Sat.
Call	x	x	x	x	x	x	x
Duration of call in min.	3	4	3	5	4	3	4
Number of self-critical statements	0	0	0	2	1	2	2
x = made call							

Figure 5.1

Observation of intervention implementation need not be complicated so that an inordinate amount of time and energy is involved. The observations should be simple, yet systematically applied to prevent unknown intervention shifts. First, specify who is to be monitored, that is, who is delivering ingredients of the intervention: worker, client, client relatives or significant others, other professionals, or employer, are examples. Second, determine who will do the monitoring. Third, decide on the contents of the intervention to be monitored. This can be done by referring to the intended efforts of the intervenors or to products that verify that interventions took place. Examples of intended efforts are the amount of time spent in interviews or sessions, types of content to discuss or to ignore in interviews, and tasks that need to be completed. Products are completed tasks that may involve compliance with such things as specified procedures, following of directions, completing assignments, or calling people.

Simple forms for indicating if the intended efforts took place or the products were produced are sufficient for monitoring whether an intervention is being implemented as planned. For instance, an intervention may call for the worker to make daily phone calls to the client, talking for 3-5 minutes about whether or not the client completed an assignment of observing the number of times he criticized himself. The worker checks daily as to whether or not the call was made, the length of the conversation, and the number of times the client said he criticized himself, on a form such as Figure 5.1. Obviously, monitoring can be burdensome, particularly if one gathers reams of information or unnecessary details. The rule of thumb is to make checklists of those ingredients that are regarded as the core of intervention, those components

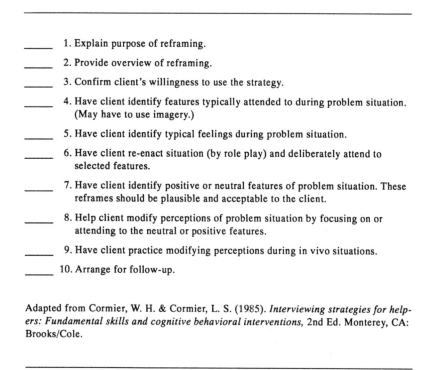

_____ 1. Explain purpose of reframing.

_____ 2. Provide overview of reframing.

_____ 3. Confirm client's willingness to use the strategy.

_____ 4. Have client identify features typically attended to during problem situation. (May have to use imagery.)

_____ 5. Have client identify typical feelings during problem situation.

_____ 6. Have client re-enact situation (by role play) and deliberately attend to selected features.

_____ 7. Have client identify positive or neutral features of problem situation. These reframes should be plausible and acceptable to the client.

_____ 8. Help client modify perceptions of problem situation by focusing on or attending to the neutral or positive features.

_____ 9. Have client practice modifying perceptions during in vivo situations.

_____ 10. Arrange for follow-up.

Adapted from Cormier, W. H. & Cormier, L. S. (1985). *Interviewing strategies for helpers: Fundamental skills and cognitive behavioral interventions,* 2nd Ed. Monterey, CA: Brooks/Cole.

Figure 5.2   Reframing Checklist

which are *sine qua non* of the planned help for the client, where it is expected that the intervention objectives would not take place if those components are not implemented.

A more elaborate monitoring device is depicted in Figure 5.2 which lists the steps for implementing reframing. A worker might develop this checklist at the same time that the intervention plan is being devised. A copy could be stored in the client's file and would serve as a reminder before each meeting with the client. As reframing steps are completed, the appropriate item would be checked. Obviously, the plan for implementing reframing and the checklist could be revised as needed.

Monitoring is particularly important when more than one person (such as the worker and the spouse) is delivering the intervention, simply because it is more likely that things will go wrong when more people are involved. Simple monitoring devices may very well ease the social worker's function of coordinating all of those persons involved in delivery of the intervention. These monitoring devices can also serve as a quick reminder to the worker of the key things to do in each session or between sessions.

IMPLEMENTATION FAILURE

Implementation failure occurs when the social worker is not able to implement the intervention as planned. This may be attributable to factors within the client system, within the system of intervenors, and/or within the interactions between the worker, the client, and extraneous events. The client may be distrustful of the worker and suspicious of the intervention. Intervention may have a low priority in the client's life; hence, such a client may miss appointments, be late for them, and/or not fully participate in the intervention plan during sessions, at related meetings, or in completing homework assignments outside of the session. Components of the intervention may be regarded as noxious or antithetical to the client's values. For instance, a client may find that an assignment to maintain a journal of her thoughts about the sexual abuse she experienced as a child is so painful that she rarely records anything other than superficial thoughts.

There may also be factors within the worker that lead to implementation failure. An intervention may be incompatible with a social worker's sense of ethics. As an example, confronting a client and pointing out failures may appear too much like punishment to some workers. They may regard this as unethical in the same manner that others might regard the use of tangible reinforcers (such as candy or coupons redeemable at fast food restaurants) as unethical. The worker may be insensitive to client needs and may not develop a sufficient degree of rapport in the relationship with the client system, thereby leading to implementation failure. Or, the worker may be forgetful or disorganized and render the interventions inconsistently.

Both worker and client may have a good working relationship, but other events may disturb the intervention plans. These include such things as accidents, illness, or family crises that affect the worker and/or the client. Or, persons involved in the treatment might be inconsistent in their degree of enthusiasm and in their completion of tasks. For example, a teacher may forget to provide daily information on a child's attendance, tardiness, and performance.

McMahon (1987) discusses a number of factors that might be responsible for treatment shift, which refers to the fact that an intervention may be implemented correctly at one point, but shifts may occur over time. These shifts may be due to fatigue, boredom, or lack of motivation to induce change. McMahon further points out that the worker may become more skilled with the intervention over time, which would result in an inconsistency in the way the intervention is delivered. She also notes that the client and worker expectancy of progress or lack of progress may influence the reliability of the intervention.

CORRECTING IMPLEMENTATION FAILURE

To adequately implement an intervention, it is necessary to monitor the behaviors of the intervenors to determine whether failure occurs. Then, the worker should attempt to determine the reasons for failure and try to overcome them.

If there appear to be problems with the intervention procedures themselves in that they are too ambiguous, then, the obvious solution is to provide more details in the procedural description, explain these details if intervenors other than the social worker are involved, and train these intervenors in the use of the interventions.

Since treatment shift or inconsistency in the implementation of treatment over time can occur with the worker and others, the worker can plan to monitor implementation on an irregular or spot-check basis over time. For example, the most salient facts about implementation might be reviewed after every other interview.

If fatigue and boredom take place, the worker might shift locations for the intervention, or reduce the time involved in an interview. The lighting in the room, the decoration, the time of day, and other factors may encourage drowsiness. A well-ventilated office decorated in light colors might be helpful for some workers. The main point here is that the worker should note the fatigue and boredom, try to determine why it is occurring, and make whatever changes are necessary so that the worker can be as helpful as possible to the client.

The worker should maintain good rapport with the client. From time to time, the worker should check on such things as her or his understanding of the client's problem and environment. By the same token, the worker should be certain that the client understands the procedures and rationale for accurate and consistent implementation of the intervention, to the extent that the client is involved in implementation.

If the intervention failure appears to be attributable to ethical problems, the worker should address this situation directly. If it is unethical to use the particular intervention, then another intervention should immediately be substituted, assuming it too has promise of achieving the desired intervention objectives. On the other hand, the worker may regard the intervention as ethical, while the client does not. The worker should explain why the intervention is considered to be appropriate. If it continues to be objectionable to the client, then the worker should not use it, showing respect to the client and preserving the relationship and client motivation so that another intervention can be attempted. The objectives of intervention and its possible success should be clearly stated and discussed at the beginning of the intervention process. Also, the worker should determine the client's expectancies regarding the intervention so they can be dealt with in a realistic manner. The possible benefits and risks of intervention should be clearly conveyed to the client, so that possible fears about what could happen as a result of intervention are minimized.

DETERMINING THE DEGREE OF CLIENT IMPROVEMENT

As the intervention is implemented, the social worker will be watching for indicators that the client is improving in the desired direction. Client implementation is reflected in variables that are relevant to the intervention objectives. If the objectives are concerned with change, the worker will look for changes in the variable(s). In contrast, maintenance and prevention objectives lead the worker to look for absence of change on those variables related to maintenance or prevention. For instance, an objective to prevent violent acts should lead to absence of violence.

Assuming that the social worker detects some improvement when examining the variable(s), a determination must be made about the degree of improvement. The worker is faced with several choices, including continue the intervention plan without any changes, revise the intervention plan, replace the intervention plan with a new one, or terminate the intervention because the objective has been accomplished. To aid in making this decision, the worker can consider the clinical significance and the statistical significance of the data reflecting progress toward achieving intervention objectives.

Clinical Significance. Improvement is progress in the direction of the intervention objective. Clinically, improvement is indicated by a reliable change in measurement of variables from one state to another. Suppose the objective is to reduce the amount of alcohol a client drinks from 8 glasses of Scotch per day to some lesser number. The intervention objective might be total abstinence, that is, no drinking, or the objective might be to drop to 1 glass of Scotch per day. Improvement is a reduction in drinking that the social worker, and perhaps the client, regard as significant given the history of the particular client's drinking behavior. It is a subjective judgment about some quantitative change in a variable.

A different criterion of clinical significance is proposed by Jacobson, Follette, and Revenstorf (1984). They suggest ". . . a change in therapy is clinically significant when the client moves from the dysfunctional to the functional range during the course of therapy on whatever variable is used to measure the clinical problem . . ." (Jacobson, Follette, & Revenstorf, 1984, p. 340). Referring to the above example of drinking behavior, the worker would have to have knowledge of the effects of drinking as well as of drinking behavior of a normative functioning group. While 8 drinks per day might be viewed as dysfunctional, only 1 drink per day may be regarded as normative for healthy, functioning adults. Therefore, obtaining the objective of 1 drink per day would be an indication of clinically significant progress.

In another example, an intervention objective might be to increase a child's level of self-esteem. The variable, self-esteem, could be measured by a standardized instrument, such as the Piers-Harris Children's Self-Concept Scale (Piers, 1984). If the child scored a 38 on this instrument before the intervention was implemented, this would indicate below-average level of self-esteem according to normative data for this instrument. Suppose that following the implementation of an intervention plan, the child scored a 53, which is in the upper end of the average range. This could be considered as clinically significant improvement.

The judgment of clinical significance is not restricted to ordinal, interval, and ratio scales, but also can be made on nominal scales showing a change of state for a particular client. The adoption of a child, release from an institution and subsequent independent living in the community, or move to a shelter for abused women are examples of nominal scale changes that might be thought of as clinically significant.

Statistical Significance. Another criterion to gauge improvement is that of statistical significance. Comparing measurements of a variable during an intervention with the measurements taken during assessment (baseline) is the basic procedure employed here. Statistical significance refers to a statistical change in the pattern of measurement at intervention from the pattern of observations at baseline, such that the probability of obtaining the measurement values at intervention is less than 5 times in 100. Thus, statistical significance signifies a rare occurrence.

Conventional values to represent this are .001, .01, .05, and sometimes .10.* Basically, the presumption is that there is no statistical significance if measurement values are the same at baseline and intervention. As the difference between intervention values and baseline values grows larger, the probability of obtaining such a difference becomes smaller and smaller.**

If the changes between baseline and intervention are statistically significant, an association between the intervention and the observed changes can be inferred. Statistically significant changes in the desired direction can indicate whether improvement or progress has occurred.

Statistical significance, however, is not identical to clinical significance. For example, the client with the drinking problem may have reduced her drinking from 8 drinks to 5 drinks per day and, when analyzed, these data may suggest a statistically significant degree of improvement. Nonetheless, this amount of change may not be sufficient for the client to be considered as functional, in the view of the social worker, the client's family, and the client's employer.

The criterion of statistical significance can be used to show a lack of change when the intervention objectives are maintenance and/or prevention. In the case of maintenance, suppose that a client changed from heavy drinking to total abstinence. A subsequent intervention plan might involve increasing the client's social support system, with an intervention objective of maintaining total abstinence. The notion of statistical significance can be used to determine whether the client deviated from nondrinking to drinking behavior.

MONITORING CLIENT IMPROVEMENT

As previously discussed, social workers should monitor the extent to which an intervention is implemented. After the implementation is successful, the worker should examine client improvement. This is done during the period of intervention to infer if the intervention is taking hold. Monitoring of improvement should occur as soon as the intervention is implemented by measuring the same variables that were measured during assessment, as well as other variables that might indicate client progress. Measurements are taken at intervals similar to those at baseline. The intervals are chosen so that they are meaningful in the

---

*For purposes of presentation, we will refer to one criterion of significance, .05
**In a subsequent section of this chapter, procedures for determining statistical significance are provided.

context of a particular client problem. As examples, family arguments might be measured daily; feelings of guilt following an abortion, daily; school performance, weekly; self-concept, weekly; and compliance to a medical regimen, daily, weekly, or monthly.

Monitoring is facilitated if the social worker has a specific period of time in which some progress is expected to occur. Observations during intervention, from the onset of intervention to that point in time by which progress should be made, can then be compared with baseline observations. As a result of monitoring, the social worker is able to judge if progress is made and make one of several practice decisions.

As was indicated in Chapter 2, variables may be reflective of different types of data, Types 1 to 4. Further, different data might be gathered in accordance with the specific objectives for a given client. Hence, degree of improvement might be observed for two or more variables. For instance, in addition to drinking behavior, a client's attitudes toward drinking and knowledge about the effects of alcohol might be measured.

Practice Decisions Related to Monitoring. Social workers must make numerous decisions about interventions for client systems. Once an intervention plan has been developed and implemented, the worker must decide whether to continue the plan, modify it, or stop it. Monitoring the extent of progress in attaining intervention objectives provides important information for making further intervention decisions.

Assuming that the social worker has routinely been collecting information with the instrument(s) selected to monitor client attainment of an objective, at some point the worker will consider the degree of progress toward the objective. As noted earlier, the point at which this occurs depends on the time frame for expected changes. For example, a change in ego functioning might not be expected to occur until several months of intervention had passed, whereas a change in child behavior as the result of introducing a new child-management technique might be expected to occur very rapidly. When the point of expected change occurs, the worker can examine the measurements to make one of the following basic inferences: attainment of intervention objectives; progress but nonattainment of objectives; no progress but nonattainment of objectives; or deterioration.

Attainment of intervention objectives signifies that the expected results, as stated in the intervention objectives, were realized. This attainment of objectives is evident in the variables being measured. The measurements are at the desired magnitude, and that magnitude is stable over time. *Progress* refers to clinical or statistical significance in terms of intervention objectives that are expected to show change on certain specified variables. In this case, change in the desired direction is noted, but the magnitude of change is not sufficient to indicate that intervention objectives were achieved. When intervention objectives are not expected to demonstrate change in variables, as is the case when objectives are focused on prevention or maintenance, change would not be expected in measurements taken during intervention as compared to baseline observations. *No progress* refers to data that show no improvement, either judged clinically or with respect to statistical significance. *Deterioration* is a condition in which there is observed change, statistically or clinically significant, but the change is opposite to that which was intended in the objective for the client.

Often in practice, there are multiple objectives for a particular client, but one intervention plan. Here, there might be different levels of progress for different variables with the same client. For example, an adult female client who is caring for her older, disabled parents may be less isolated from other family members and peers, and no longer experiencing insomnia, but she may still have strong feelings of anger and resentment toward her parents. Where there are multiple objectives, the decision making involves a complex set of possibilities which are guided by the worker's judgment about which objective is most important, as well as the context in which the intervention is imbedded. For purposes of presentation, we will consider several intervention decisions, but in relation to one intervention objective. Our purpose here is not to suggest inflexible decisions that should be employed in all situations. Rather, the attempt is to illustrate how monitoring information can bear on intervention decisions.

Possible decisions about interventions, once implemented, are: continue the intervention; modify the intervention; or stop the intervention. Clearly, evidence of progress would call for continuing the intervention if the progress was judged to be occurring in a timely fashion.

If progress is not occurring at an appropriate rate, the worker may consider modifying the intervention. One type of modification involves subtracting one or more components of the intervention. Suppose the intervention includes separate interviews with an individual and his family. The intervention could be changed by cancelling the family interviews or by having only joint interviews including both the individual and the family. Another way to modify the intervention is to change the way in which intervention is carried out, but not actually change the intervention methods. This might involve such things as an increase or decrease in contact hours or length of interview time, or in the intensity of the intervention. For example, a social worker using gestalt therapy might make less use of his or her own experiences in the moment during the sessions. Or, another worker using cognitive techniques might devote more of each session to helping a client dispute his irrational beliefs about his need to be loved by everyone. Other interventions could be added to the current intervention plan.

For example, a social worker attempting to improve a client's self-image by helping him recognize and acknowledge his positive accomplishments might add an intervention of having the client write and periodically review a list of his accomplishments. An informal peer support group might be added to the intervention plan for another client who is receiving a problem-solving intervention to help her leave an abusive spouse. In adding interventions, the compatibility of the new intervention with the former intervention plan must be considered.

Stopping an intervention is necessary if the worker realizes that it is actually harming the client, and if the risks from continuing the intervention actually outweigh the benefits that might accrue. An intervention should also be stopped if it is offensive to and incompatible with a client's values. Finally, if there is evidence of deterioration or no improvement after waiting a sufficient time, an intervention should be discontinued. Options that the worker can consider at this point are making a referral, conducting another assessment, seeking consultation, or devising a new intervention plan. Prior to deciding to change intervention procedures for a client, the worker should review all the available information about the problem, the implementation of the intervention, and the measurement of progress, searching for any clues that explain the deterioration or lack of progress. Discussions with the client might also be helpful.

Referral would be indicated if the client-worker relationship is actually impeding progress or if the worker knows of another agency or professional who might be better able to help the client. Conducting another assessment is in order if it appears that the initial assessment of the client's problems was inaccurate or the problem hierarchy was faulty. A new assessment, in turn, might suggest a different intervention plan.

Consultation with other colleagues, supervisors, or agency consultants might help to identify reason(s) why the intervention is not working as planned. Consultation might result in any of the above options — referral, a reassessment, a revised intervention plan, or an entirely new intervention.

TECHNIQUES FOR EVALUATING PROGRESS

Measures obtained on the dependent variable(s) that are related to intervention objectives are reviewed to evaluate progress. As previously indicated, data collected during intervention, or observations, are compared to observations representing the baseline. Techniques for evaluating these data for indications of progress include both nonstatistical and statistical methods. Only statistical methods estimate statistical significance, whereas either nonstatistical or statistical methods can be employed to infer clinical significance. Rather than provide a comprehensive review of all possible techniques, our purpose here is to present what we regard as procedures that are easy-to-use, representative of most techniques, and applicable to a range of clinical situations. Accordingly, the use of interviews and graphic analysis are described under the category of nonstatistical procedures, and three relatively straightforward statistical techniques are presented under the category of statistical procedures.

NONSTATISTICAL PROCEDURES

Interviews and Observations. Qualitative data are data in a form that are not yet translatable into measurement scales. These data typically are in narrative form and are obtainable from observations of clients or from client responses to open-ended questions in interviews and/or questionnaires. They can be easily transformed into nominal scale measurements and are suitable for determining if a problem exists at a particular point in time.

To evaluate progress with qualitative data, there are at least three different types of observations which social workers can make in the normal course of their contact with clients during intervention. These are observations of general progress, observations of changes in state, and observations of disruptions in a series of data.

To obtain information about *general progress,* the worker can directly approach the subject with the client. This might involve reviewing the agreed-upon objectives with the client and asking to what extent the client feels that progress has been made in achieving the objectives. The client may elaborate, and the social worker can probe to develop fuller understanding of the type and amount of progress, as viewed by the client. This information is combined with the worker's own observations of the client over the course of intervention, and an inference is made regarding whether or not progress has occurred.

If the worker wants to obtain data that more readily translate into nominal measurement, a question such as "Did you make progress in achieving your goals?" can be posed. Other relevant data about general progress can be obtained by asking these types of questions: "Since you began treatment, has anything impeded or aided your progress?" or "Have you made any basic changes in your life style since you began treatment?"

In situations in which the worker does not directly reveal treatment objectives to the client, questioning obviously will be less directly focused on goals. Moreover, we realize that workers are continually gathering information that addresses the issue of general progress, as well as more specific changes. The point here is that it is important to systematically ask these questions and make a judgment based on all the relevant information.

Changes of state refer to obvious behavioral, cognitive, or emotional changes that are deemed as clinically significant. They represent difficult transitions for the client and are the focus of intervention. In contrast to more general, long-range goals, changes of state often are instrumental. Some examples of changes of state that may be clinically significant for clients are: relinquishing a baby for adoption; filing for a divorce; acknowledging painful feelings regarding the loss of a close relative; confronting an adversary; or recognizing a tendency to focus on negative thoughts. Again, in an interview the worker can ask the client if these changes have occurred. Supplementary information will come from the worker's observations, or significant others who know the client. All available information is processed by the worker in an effort to determine if a change in state that can be regarded as progress has occurred during the delivery of intervention.

Disruptions in a series of data refers to a change from the baseline period when there was a stable, non-fluctuating pattern suggesting either presence of negative behaviors, cognitions, or feelings, or absence of positive behaviors, cognitions, or feelings. Clients may drink every day, make verbally abusive comments to family members daily, never leave their house, not attempt to seek employment, as examples. A disruption in this data pattern might be observed by the worker, or communicated by the client or a significant other. If a change apparently occurs, the worker should determine that it is not a one-time aberration. It also may be informative to analyze what led to the change, as this may help in maintaining the change or in stimulating other changes.

As should be apparent from the above discussion, much of what normally occurs in practice yields a rich supply of qualitative data. By systematically and routinely attempting to collect and analyze these

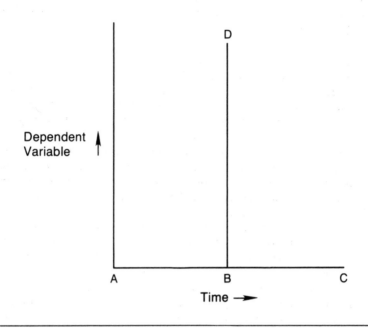

Figure 5.3

data, particularly in terms of client objectives, workers can capitalize on this information to assist them in making practice decisions. More detailed information on applications of qualitative data is available in Filstead (1978) and Tripodi (1983).

Graphic Analysis. To estimate progress by analyzing graphs of client data, the worker must gather multiple observations on one or more dependent variables, both before and during intervention. These variables relate to things that were supposed to be changed or prevented from being changed during the course of intervention. These observations are plotted on a graph with the *y*-axis representing the dependent variable and the *x*-axis signifying time, as in Figure 5.3.

Observations to the left of line BD in Figure 5.3 represent the baseline, while those to the right indicate observations taken on the dependent variable during the period of intervention.

Although there are no precise rules to follow for graphic analysis, suggestions have been made regarding what factors should be considered (Jayaratne, Tripodi, & Talsma, 1988; Parsonson & Baer, 1978). The object of analyzing graphed data in monitoring progress is to infer if there are any changes in the dependent variable during intervention as compared to the baseline pattern. These steps can be followed in analyzing patterns on graphs:

1. *Keep in mind the intervention objectives and expectations for the dependent variable during intervention.* For example, does the treatment objective call for the dependent variable to increase or decrease, if change in the client's functioning is expected? In contrast, if the intervention is preventive, no relative change would be expected in the intervention phase relative to the baseline observations.

2. *The units on the y-axis representing possible measurement levels of the dependent variable and the units on the x-axis signifying time intervals should be meaningful with respect to the clinical problem.* Recall from Chapter 3 that units can easily be inflated or contracted on graphs, resulting in distorted visual images. Because comparisons are to be made from intervention to baseline, the time units for baseline and intervention should be identical for ease of interpretation. For example, if observations are made daily during baseline, they also should be made daily during intervention.

3. *If at all possible, the social worker should define clinical significance for the particular client in relation to the dependent variable that is graphed.* This will provide a frame of reference with which to interpret the graphic patterns.

4. *Describe the baseline pattern in reference to the number of observations or measurements of the dependent variable, the magnitude of the observations, the trend in the line connecting all the observations, and the extent to which the line is stable or variable.* The more observations, the smoother the line is likely to be, and the easier it will be to analyze. At a minimum, there should be 3–5 observations. The magnitude or level of each observation is the height of the ordinate, from the x-axis to the observed magnitude demarcated on the y-axis.

There are three possible trends: *upwards or accelerating, downwards or decelerating,* and *horizontal or non-changing.* Referring to Figure 5.4, line AB shows an upward trend. With successive measurements over time, the magnitude of the dependent variable increases. Line EF is decelerating with the magnitude decreasing over time, and line CD shows no change in magnitude.

The lines in Figure 5.4 are stable, showing no deviation among observations and from the geometric representation of a straight line. In Figure 5.5, lines A, B, and C represent acceleration, no change, and deceleration, respectively. None of the graphs are stable, however, since there are deviations among the measurements and the resulting graphs do not show clear geometric expressions of a mathematical relationship (such as a straight line or an ellipse).

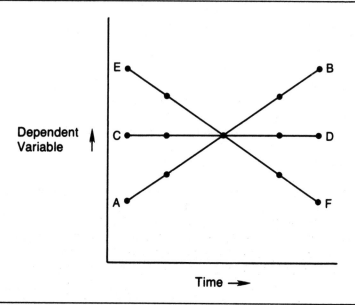

Figure 5.4

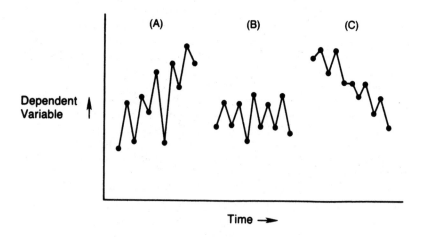

Figure 5.5

Using the above concepts, a particular baseline pattern could be described, as a horizontal line showing stability and no change at a magnitude of X with 5 observations, for example.

5. *Describe the pattern of the observations during intervention, using the same concepts as in Step 4 above.*

6. *Compare the intervention pattern with the baseline pattern of observations, looking for changes or similarities.* Compare patterns in terms of magnitude, trend, and stability or variability. Keep in mind the number of observations made and how this can influence apparent stability. Make a judgment as to whether the baseline and intervention patterns are similar or different, representing change or no change.

Figures 5.6, 5.7, and 5.8 represent stable graphs at baseline and intervention with 5 observations at baseline and at intervention. They reflect some illustrative patterns where magnitude and trend vary. In Figure 5.6, the baseline, line AB, is horizontally stable. If an increase in the dependent variable is expected, lines C_1D_1 and C_2D_2 show change. Whereas C_2D_2 shows an increase in magnitude that is stable, C_1D_1 shows an increasing or accelerating trend. Line C_3D_3 shows no change and lines C_4D_4 and C_5D_5 would show deterioration or change in an undesired direction. For the same figure, if no change is expected, line C_3D_3 would show progress consistent with the intervention objective, while all other lines would show change, or lack of progress.

Figure 5.7 shows an accelerating pattern at baseline. If an increase in magnitude is desired, line C_1E shows no change because it is following the same trend that was initiated at baseline. Hence, it provides no evidence of progress whereas line C_1D does indicate progress because there is a greater acceleration than was apparent at baseline. Lines C_2F and C_2G indicate deterioration or lack of progress. If, in Figure 5.7, it is expected that the dependent variable will decrease, then lines C_2F and C_2G indicate progress, while lines C_1D and C_1E show lack of progress.

In Figure 5.8, the baseline, AB, shows a deceleration. Line C_2F follows this same trend at intervention, showing no change. Depending on the intervention objectives, lines C_1D, C_1E, and C_2G, can be interpreted as either change (if the objective is to maintain the downward trend), progress, or deterioration.

STATISTICAL PROCEDURES

To employ statistical analyses with multiple observations of the same dependent variable, taken across baseline and intervention periods, it is necessary to have a large number of observations that are independent

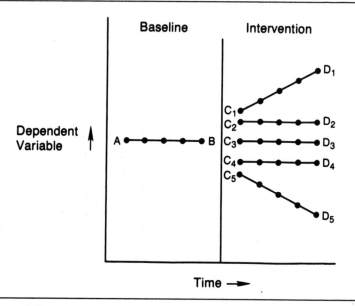

Figure 5.6

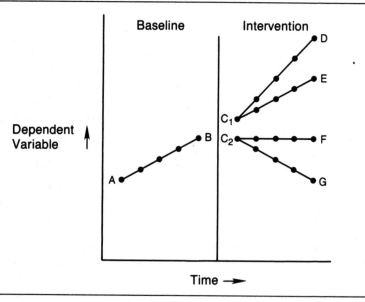

Figure 5.7

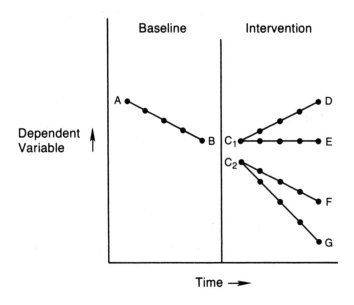

Figure 5.8

from each other and that fulfill the assumptions of the particular statistical distribution that is used for the testing (such as the binomial, normal, or chi-square distributions). These distributions and a number of statistical tests are described in standard texts on statistics (see, for example, Hays, 1973). With data gathered in practice, rarely are all of the assumptions for statistical testing met. Most difficult to obtain are large numbers of observations meeting the assumption of noncorrelation at baseline. Since many of these observations are based on reports of clients, workers, or significant others over time, it also is difficult to rule out all sources of possible bias as influencing subsequent measures. For example, a couple's responses to an instrument assessing their sexual satisfaction may be influenced by their recollections of the responses they gave when they completed the same instrument the previous week. Keeping these concerns in mind, statistical procedures can be employed to serve as a rough criterion of change. If there is a shift in the pattern of observations from baseline to intervention as defined by statistically significant changes, there is some evidence of an association between intervention and the change. The exact probabilities may not be the same as indicated by the statistical test, if the assumptions of that test are not fulfilled. Thus, statistical testing is more appropriately seen in this context as a rule-of-thumb, or an indication of whether or not there is a shift in observations from baseline to intervention.

We are presenting three statistical procedures that can be used for estimating whether there is a shift in data patterns. They are derived from procedures described by Gottman and Leiblum (1974) and Siegel (1956). These three procedures and others are described in detail in Bloom and Fischer (1982). Also, Jayaratne (1978) describes other statistical procedures.

Shewart Chart. The Shewart Chart approach proposed by Gottman and Leiblum (1974) involves the following steps:

1. Compute the mean and standard deviation of the observations at baseline. Refer to Chapter 3 where these calculations are described in detail.
2. Multiply the standard deviation by 2.
3. Add the result obtained in Step 2 to the mean. This represents $\bar{0} + 2SD$.
4. Subtract the result obtained in Step 2 from the mean. This represents $\bar{0} - 2SD$.
5. Turning to the graph containing these data, draw two straight lines that are horizontal to the x-axis and intersect points on the y-axis at $\bar{0} \pm 2SD$.
6. Extend these lines into the intervention phase, as shown in Figure 5.9.

The extended (dotted) lines of $\bar{0} \pm 2SD$ are the lines of the Shewart Chart. Any observations during the intervention period that occur within the lines are not statistically different from the magnitude of observations during baseline. If observations occur outside of the shaded region (indicating that they are greater than $\bar{0} \pm 2SD$ or less than $\bar{0} - 2SD$), these observations are said to be statistically significant if the assumptions for obtaining a normal distribution are met. Statistical significance can be interpreted as meaning that the chances of these observations occurring outside of the shaded region are less than 5 in 100. Gottman and Leiblum (1974) also include a procedure for testing for autocorrelation. We consider this to be unnecessary so long as the statistical test is only regarded as a rough criterion of whether or not there is an association between the intervention and shifts in data patterns.

To illustrate an application of this procedure, suppose that a teenage client was truant from school for 3 days a week for 3 weeks in a row, then 5 days a week for the next 3 weeks in a row. After the 6th week, an intervention involving the child's family was instituted. Observations of days truant for 6 weeks of intervention are 5, 5, 3, 2, 1, and 0.

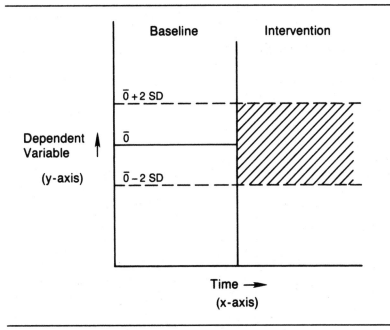

Figure 5.9

The Shewart procedure can be carried out to determine if there is evidence of an association between the intervention and the number of days truant. The graph and necessary computations are shown in Figure 5.10.

As is apparent from Figure 5.10, there was a dramatic reversal in the client's truancy shortly after the family was involved in treatment. Assuming the intervention objective is to reduce the number of truancies, the analysis suggests that statistical significance is reached in weeks 11 and 12, when the number of truancies drops below the Shewart line of 1.8. Thus, there is evidence of progress, and the social worker should be encouraged to extend the intervention and to observe whether the teenager continues to attend all classes, as he did in week 12.

Binomial Test for Horizontal Baselines. The binomial is one of the most widely used statistics and is fully described in standard statistical texts. Siegel (1956) showed that it could be used as the basis for a variety of statistical tests in many practical situations and that it has fewer mathematical assumptions than does the normal curve, which is the basic distribution for the Shewart Chart procedure.

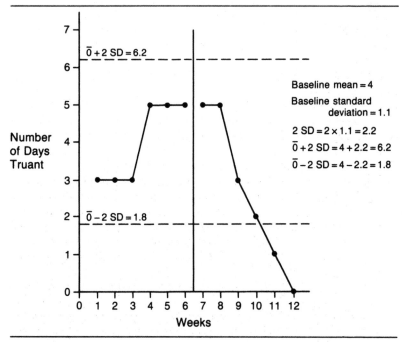

Figure 5.10

We illustrate the use of the binomial for two different types of baseline trends, the first of which is horizontal. A horizontal baseline is one that depicts relatively stable observations that can be represented by a straight line. For example, Figure 5.11 shows a cyclic pattern that is horizontal at baseline. This test can be used for determining progress, if the assumption that intervention is equally likely to be associated with success or failure can be accepted. To determine statistical significance at or beyond the .05 level with the binomial test (that is, where the chances of observations occurring are 5 or less in 100), at least 5 observations must be collected during intervention.

The procedure for using the binomial to determine success is as follows:

1. The median of the baseline observations is calculated (6 in this example), and a straight line representing the median is extended into the intervention period.

2. Determine whether success is indicated by observations that fall above or below the median. In this example, success is defined as observations occurring during intervention below the median, and failure defined as

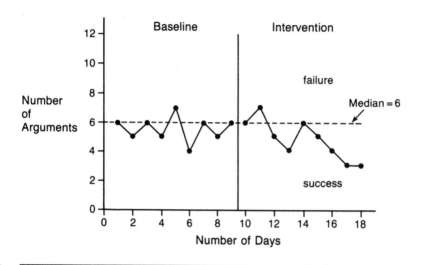

Figure 5.11

observations occurring above the median. Thus, any observation below 6 would be regarded as indicating a success, since it would be consistent with an intervention objective of reducing the number of arguments between spouses.

3. Count the number of observations and the number of successes. There are 9 observations, and 6 successes in Figure 5.11. The observations falling on the median are not counted as successes.

4. Refer to Table 5.1. Locate the column for the number of observations, and refer to the number 9.

5. Reading across that row, locate the minimum number of successes required. This number is 8. Hence, if 8 successes are obtained for 9 observations, there is an association between the intervention and reduction in arguments. No association can be inferred from the data in Figure 5.11.

This Binomial Test can be used after intervention is underway or after the baseline has been completed but before intervention is started. In the latter case, the binomial would indicate how many successes would be necessary to conclude that there is an association between the intervention and the observed success, after X observations. As can be seen in Table 5.1, all of the observations must be successful when there are 5, 6, or 7 observations; for higher numbers, fewer successes are required, but the number is still high. For example, 20 observations would require 15 successes.

Table 5.1 Minimum Number of Successes for Statistical Significance at $p \leq .05$

Number of Observations During Intervention	Minimum Number of Successes Required
5*	5
6	6
7	7
8	7
9	8
10	9
11	9
12	10
13	11
14	11
15	12
16	12
17	13
18	14
19	14
20	15
21	16
22	16
23	17
24	17
25	18

*NOTE: This is the smallest number of observations for which statistical significance can be evaluated.

SOURCE: Derived and adapted from Table IV, B, of Walker, Helen and Lev, J. (1953). *Statistical Inference.* New York: Holt, p. 458, which reports probabilities associated with observed values in the binomial test.

Celeration Line Technique. The final technique to be presented is the Celeration Line. This is a revised version from that described by Gingerich and Feyerherm (1979), such that it is procedurally similar to the Binomial Test for Horizontal Baselines presented above. In conception, the Celeration Line technique applies the Binomial Test to accelerating or decelerating trend lines.

The procedures to be followed are:

1. Plot the baseline observations on a graph. According to Gingerich and Feyerherm (1979), there should be a minimum of 10 baseline observations, although other writers indicate that 7 is sufficient (Bloom & Fischer, 1982).

2. Divide the baseline into half and calculate the median for each half.

3. Divide each half in half again, constructing a line perpendicular to the *x*-axis at each of those points. The line closest to the *y*-axis is the ¼ line; the other is the ¾ line.

4. Plot the computed median value for the first half on the ¼ line, and for the second half on the ¾ line. Connect those two points to form a straight line, which is the celeration line.

5. Extend the straight line into the intervention phase.

6. Decide whether successful interventions are defined as points falling above, below, or on the celeration line, in relation to intervention objectives.

7. Count the number of observations in intervention. There should be a minimum of 5, but it is preferable that the number of observations be similar to the number in the baseline period. Determine the number of observations that can be considered successes, eliminating from consideration those points that fall exactly on the line since they are neither successes nor failures (unless success is defined as falling on the line).

8. Use the values in Step 7 above and refer to Table 5.1 to determine whether there is a statistically significant change.

This procedure is illustrated in Figure 5.12. Referring to Figure 5.12, the median for the first half is 15 arguments and that point is plotted on the ¼ line; the median of 13 for the second half is plotted on the ¾ line. Connecting those points and extending the line forms the celeration line. With the line in Figure 5.12, it is apparent that there can be observations above or below the line for the next 10 observations. If the trend of the celeration line is so steep that it intersects the x-axis before the observation period ends, however, then the Celeration Line technique cannot be used since the observations would not have an equally likely chance of occurring above or below the line.

Suppose the intervention objective is to reduce the number of arguments further than is evident in the downward trend of the celeration line. From Table 5.1, we know that if 9 observations during intervention were above the celeration line and only 1 was below, there would be a statistically significant shift in the observations from baseline to intervention, but in a direction opposite to that which was desired. This would indicate that there is not only lack of progress, but deterioration that is associated with the intervention. This would call for the worker to consider whether the intervention should be stopped or modified. In fact, there were only 8 points below the celeration line, which is not sufficient to indicate statistically significant change.

There are some limitations to the Celeration Line technique that need to be considered. These are:

1. The ¼ and ¾ lines may not be adequate points to reflect the trend when there is a great deal of variability among the observations.

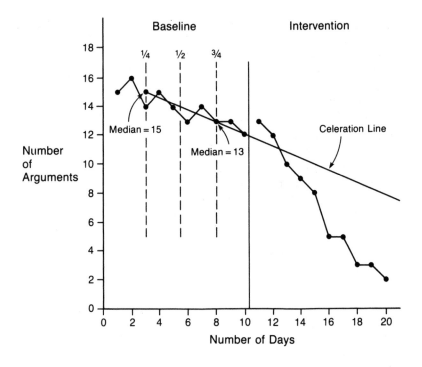

Figure 5.12

2. The celeration line would not be appropriate if it is not possible to obtain observations that can fall either above or below the celeration line during the intervention period (because the trend is too steep).

3. At least 7-10 observations should be made at baseline, and preferably the same number during intervention. With smaller numbers of observations, it is difficult, if not impossible, to observe accurate trends.

4. The assumptions of equally likely observations may not be tenable. Instead, even steeper (more acceleration over time for an accelerating trend and more deceleration for a decelerating trend) might be assumed.

Like the Binomial Test for Horizontal Baselines, this technique can be used once the baseline period is over to determine the number of successful observations that are necessary to determine statistically significant progress.

EXERCISES

1. Define and discuss the concepts of treatment integrity and procedural reliability as they relate to an intervention you are using for a particular client. Describe the intervention in as much detail as possible.

2. Devise a simple form to use for monitoring a specific intervention for a client.

3. Discuss possible sources of implementation failure for either of the interventions described in numbers 1 or 2 above.

4. For a particular client, specify intervention objectives and describe the intervention. Describe how you might evaluate progress for that client by nonstatistical techniques.

5. Devise a graph to show how you could evaluate progress by comparing observations during intervention with baseline observations for a client group. Describe the trends in the data. Discuss how you might use either Shewart Chart analysis or the Binomial Test to estimate statistical significance.

Chapter 6

TERMINATION AND FOLLOW-UP

The final step in a problem-solving process of intervention with clients involves a planned termination of the intervention. Follow-up has the function of determining whether or not the client has maintained gains achieved during the intervention, as well as assessing the extent to which the client is in further need of intervention, either for problems for which intervention was delivered or for new problems that arise.

TERMINATION

Termination is the cessation of intervention activity. Its occurrence is planned by the social worker and/or the client. Obviously, client dropout is an unplanned termination, which may be due to a variety of possible reasons such as dissatisfaction, lack of motivation or resources, and unsuitable appointment times. In contrast, planned termination is a conscious decision made by the social worker, ideally in cooperation with the client, to discontinue the intervention process. If the intervention objectives are achieved and there are no other problems to work on, termination may be planned by the social worker. Such terminations, of course, are able to be effectuated in open settings where there are no mandatory restrictions on the client as there possibly are in other settings, such as correctional or medical long-term care facilities.

Social workers might plan termination even where there is no progress, or possibly deterioration. For example, a decision might be made to refer the client to other resources, especially if the social worker has exhausted her or his repertoire of interventions and decided that other workers in the agency would not be any more effective with this particular client.

Two basic types of planned terminations are:

1. termination of an intervention, or the focus of an intervention; or
2. termination of the case.

Termination of an intervention or the focus of an intervention occurs when the social worker ceases to administer an intervention that focuses on a particular problem or objective, while continuing to provide different interventions or the same intervention focused on different client problems and/or objectives. This type of termination occurs while contact is continued with the client.

The second type of planned termination is the termination of a case. This involves the planned withdrawal of any worker, intervention, or contact with the client.

This chapter will be devoted to the use of measurement principles and concepts in securing information about client progress following both types of termination. Therefore, both follow-up during client contact and follow-up after intervention are discussed.

FOLLOW-UP

Follow-up is the acquisition of information about the client's level of functioning in relation to intervention objectives after an intervention is no longer administered or all intervention has been terminated.

Why should follow-up take place? When there are so few resources available in social agencies, why not simply use them to deliver as many services as possible to those who are referred for or seek agency services? There are at least three interrelated reasons for engaging in follow-up activities. First, it is important to determine whether the client functions well without intervention and to be able to offer continued help if it is so desired and needed. This is an ethical position that maintains that clients have a right to treatment and that there should be continuity in treatment over time. Second, it is important to determine the extent to which interventions are effective. This is necessary practice knowledge that enables social workers to be accountable to the profession, the community, and their clients. Third, follow-up may be a planned part of intervention, with the purpose of follow-up serving as a context for continual assessment in relation to whether or not intervention needs to be reinstituted. The client may need a booster session with the social worker to reinforce further the possible achievements made during an intervention. With respect to intervention objectives, there are several possible outcomes that might be discerned during follow-up:

1. The client may be functioning at the same level in follow-up as at termination. That is, there would be no clinically or statistically significant changes from termination to follow-up.

2. The client may have shown more improvement since termination. This may be attributable to an improvement trend that commenced before termination, a delayed intervention effect, or to other, nonintervention factors that might have been responsible for improvement.

3. There may be a gradual deterioration that is a result of premature withdrawal of the intervention or of other unknown factors.

4. Rather than a gradual deterioration, there may be a complete relapse. An example is a recovered addict who is drug-free for a long period but relapses on one occasion and then resumes his or her former drug habit.

FOLLOW-UP DURING CLIENT CONTACT

Follow-up during client contact refers to follow-up during the first type of termination described above; that is, the social worker terminates one intervention or the focus of one intervention, and then either applies that intervention to another objective for that client or continues to administer another intervention for a different objective for the same client. For purposes of illustration, suppose there are two objectives for a teenage mother: (1) use of contraceptives; and (2) attendance in high school classes. For the first objective, the intervention may consist of attending a weekly discussion group with her peers and led by the social worker. A behavioral technique based on positive reinforcement might be used to help her achieve the second objective, school attendance. Now, suppose that both interventions are delivered simultaneously. The objectives might be regarded as accomplished if there is continued progress for two months. If the school attendance objective is attained, the social worker may terminate the reinforcement intervention, but still have the adolescent attend the discussion group.

Or, another possibility is that the positive reinforcement is the only intervention employed by the worker to accomplish both objectives. If one of the objectives is attained, the positive reinforcement might be discontinued for that objective, and follow-up could ensue. Meanwhile, the reinforcement program would continue for the other objective until some progress was evident.

Still another possibility is the sequential, rather than the simultaneous, application of interventions. The group discussion may be administered for the birth control objective. After that objective is attained, either the discussion group could address the client's school attendance problem, or the client could stop attending the discussion group and a reinforcement program could be directed toward increasing school attendance. Meanwhile, follow-up would center on the client's use of birth control.

INFORMATION

Information to gather for follow-up is basically the same as that gathered for monitoring purposes. Data should be pertinent to intervention objectives and subject to graphic and/or statistical analyses as described in the previous chapter. These data are quantitative and measurable by nominal, ordinal, interval, or ratio scales. In addition, qualitative data, which have not been translated into any of the measurement scales, may inform the follow-up effort. Qualitative data, obtained from such sources as the client, or the client's employment, school, or significant others serve to enrich descriptions of what is happening to the client and to what extent the client has changed to or maintained adequate functioning. Moreover, it provides clues as to why interventions appear to succeed or fail, possible aids or hindrances to the further implementation of interventions, and additional ideas regarding an assessment of the client. Such information is obtained by the worker's observations and interviews of others who have observed the client's functioning.

Although there are no precise guidelines regarding when to gather data during follow-up, several factors should be considered. First, the social worker should review information about the client's history, the patterns of data for the client at baseline and intervention periods, and the intervention objectives. Besides shedding light on the question of timing of follow-up, this review will provide ideas about the basic information that should be sought. For example, if the client has a history of alcoholism, regardless of whether the current intervention objectives were focused on drinking behaviors, the social worker might seek information during follow-up that would identify any dramatic change or relapse with regard to drinking. Second, the specificity of the intervention objectives may indicate expectations regarding the maintenance of any change(s) achieved during intervention. Third, the social worker can form opinions as to what would be critical periods of follow-up time in which there might be deterioration and, accordingly, collect data at those time points. Fourth, the decision as to when to collect data should be practical. Since work is still being done with the client on other treatment objectives, the worker will have the opportunity to gather information at every client contact, as a general rule. Fifth, if the worker has knowledge of the natural history of the variables measured over time (such as delinquency, child abuse, heroin addiction, or verbal aggression) or access to literature that conceptualizes and/or reports empirical data on those phenomena, this information can guide the schedule for obtaining measurements.

If it is not too time-consuming, it is preferable to gather data at similar time points as at baseline and follow-up. This, of course, assumes that the data gathering is brief (for example, 5 minutes or less of a 60-minute interview), which is likely to be so for quantitative data. Information that is not directly related to the intervention objectives and is qualitative in nature should be obtained less frequently (such as every fifth interview, if there is a week or more between interviews).

ANALYZING DATA

Follow-up data should be analyzed to determine if the client maintained the gains realized during intervention and if the data patterns continue to be stable. The basic format for graphing follow-up data is depicted in Figure 6.1.

Data are plotted for baseline, intervention, and follow-up. To analyze data for progress, the method described in Chapter 5 for comparing intervention data to baseline data can be employed. Follow-up data can be compared to either baseline or intervention data. Graphically, one can simply observe trends and changes in trends, if they emerge, from baseline to intervention and from intervention to follow-up. One could also compare follow-up data with those at baseline to estimate the client's functioning at that time compared to functioning prior to intervention. In Figure 6.1, during intervention, there is an increase in magnitude which is similar to the trend of the last two data points at baseline, and which stabilizes horizontally during follow-up. At follow-up, the magnitude is slightly increased from intervention, but is much greater than at baseline. *In short, there were changes to an increased magnitude, and they were maintained at follow-up after intervention was terminated.*

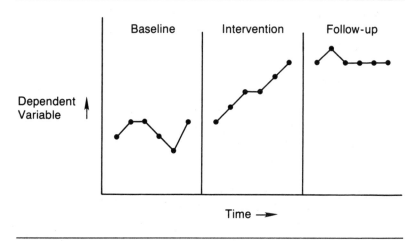

Figure 6.1

For statistical analyses, the procedures described in Chapter 5 are followed. To compare follow-up with intervention, the intervention period would be treated as the benchmark (baseline). Thus, the mean ±2 standard deviations in Shewart Chart analysis would be calculated for data during intervention. If follow-up is to be compared with baseline, then in Shewart Chart analysis, the mean ±2 standard deviations would be calculated for baseline data, and the lines would be extended into the follow-up period. Observations falling above the mean plus two standard deviations and below the mean minus two standard deviations would be statistically significant.

Calculation of the binomial and use of Celeration Line techniques would follow the same procedures. When comparing follow-up to intervention, intervention data serve as the benchmark (baseline); and baseline data form the benchmark when comparing baseline with either intervention or follow-up data.

INFERENCES FROM DATA PATTERNS

Graphic patterns and the use of statistical significance can provide evidence of an association between the intervention and changes in the data for the dependent variables. This is especially plausible if the data indicate there is a problem at baseline while no intervention is present and the problem is significantly reduced after the introduction of the intervention. After the intervention is terminated and the follow-up data pattern is compared with that at intervention, the following inferences can be made:

1. If there is no change between intervention and follow-up, progress has been maintained.
2. If there are significant negative changes between intervention and follow-up, progress has not been maintained.
3. If there are significant positive changes between intervention and follow-up, there continues to be progress but without intervention.

The interpretation of data is ambiguous and inconclusive for the previously mentioned possibility of follow-up during on-going client contact when one intervention is used simultaneously to accomplish two different objectives and, upon achievement of one of the objectives, is no longer focused on that objective. In this instance, it may be difficult to argue that no intervention occurs during follow-up, since worker contact with the client continues and the same intervention is used on another objective. Hence, interpretations regarding follow-up would not be as clear as they are for other instances of follow-up during client contact.

To what extent is it possible to say that the intervention is not only associated with significant changes, but is also responsible for those changes? Or, put in a different way, is there a causal relationship between intervention and progress or maintenance of progress?

To answer this, it is first necessary to indicate what evidence is needed to infer causal relationships. A causal relationship is one in which changes in one or more independent variables lead to changes in one or more dependent variables. There may be a complex set of interrelating factors, which in combination are responsible for observed changes in dependent variables. For purposes of presentation, however, let us consider the requisites for a simple causal relationship between an intervention and a specified outcome of that intervention.

First, changes in the intervention must precede changes in the outcome. Stated differently, a causal relationship cannot be inferred if the client began to accomplish the intervention objective prior to the introduction of the intervention.

Second, there must be a significant association between the intervention and the outcome. This might be manifest in one of the following ways, as examples:

a. There are statistically significant differences between the average level of the dependent variable when intervention is in place as opposed to when intervention is not being delivered.

b. There is a statistically significant correlation between the independent and the dependent variable.

c. There is a correlation of a sufficient magnitude to result in a high degree of predictability. The square of the correlation coefficient multiplied by 100 is an index of predictability in terms of percentage. A correlation of .3 has 9% predictability; .5, 25%; and .7, 49%. (Tripodi, 1983, pp. 86-87)

Third, there must be no factors other than the intervention that lead to changes in the outcome. These other factors are called *internal validity threats* by Campbell and Stanley (1963), and several research texts expand these factors and discuss possible ways in which these factors can be controlled by experimental research designs (see, for example, Bloom & Fisher, 1982, Cook & Campbell, 1979, and Barlow & Hersen, 1984). Threats to internal validity that might affect causal relationships for a single client with repeated measurements over time include factors such as these:

a. *History* — Variables that occur between different measurements of the dependent variable over time. These can include any of a range of events such as loss of a job, marriage, or the onset of winter weather.

b. *Maturation* — Variables referring to physical changes within clients over time such as illness, developmental growth, or fatigue.

c. *Initial measurement effects* — Subsequent responses to a measuring device that were affected by responses to the first measurement.

d. *Instrumentation* — The process of measurement is unstandardized and results in a change in the dependent variable. For instance, instrumentation effects might occur when a role-play test of social skill is administered with a male confederate on one occasion and a female confederate on another.

e. *Statistical regression* — The tendency for more extreme scores to regress to more average scores on repeated measurements of a dependent variable.

f. *Multiple treatment interference* — Clients are receiving interventions from sources other than the one the social worker is evaluating. These other interventions may be responsible for changes in dependent variables.

g. *Expectancy effects* — Clients may show change on the basis of their expectations regarding the intervention, the social worker's skill, and other such factors.

h. *Interactions* — Combined effects of any of the previous factors.

i. *Other factors* — There are other unknown variables that explain the occurrence of change in dependent variables.

This list of internal validity threats is geared to a single client. Obviously, the number and types of potential threats increase as intervention is directed toward families and groups. One can never be absolutely confident about a causal relationship to the extent that it can be shown that no other factors, such as those listed, are responsible for the outcome. In short, a causal relationship can only be inferred. Don't despair! Causal knowledge can be approximated. Demonstrating a time-ordered relationship between the intervention and the dependent variable, and having clinically and/or statistically significant changes that are consistent with intervention objectives is a good start. Stable, horizontal, baseline patterns and standard measurement procedures control for initial measurement effects, instrumentation, and statistical regression. And, the absence of history, maturation, multiple treatment interference and expectancy effects might be inferred from qualitative information obtained from observations and interviews in the course of working with the client. For example, it may be clear that a client has reduced his violent behavior as determined by clear, consistent data patterns with statistically and clinically significant changes observed. Qualitative information may indicate there have been no changes in the client's environment, family structure, physical health, or expectancies about intervention (the client expected little change in this case). In addition, the client appears to be receiving no interventions from other resources. In this example, causality is not demonstrated empirically, but can be inferred. If internal validity threats appear to be minimized, the causal influence of the intervention is plausible for that particular case and intervention. If the social worker uses the same intervention with other clients experiencing similar problems and the results continually show the accomplishment of intervention objectives, it becomes increasingly plausible to infer a causal relationship.

RELATED PRACTICE DECISIONS

In general, practice decisions that might be made when conducting follow-up for the effects of an intervention while still maintaining contact with the client involve continuation of monitoring, discontinuance of follow-up, or reinstitution of intervention. If there is no change from intervention to follow-up, the maintenance of intervention objectives is indicated. The social worker may continue monitoring at regular intervals if it seems likely that the client will show deterioration on the dependent variable. On the other hand, continued progress that exceeds the intervention objectives may indicate to the worker that monitoring is no longer necessary. Gradual deterioration or relapse demand that the worker consider reinstating the intervention or combining the initial intervention with another intervention, with continued monitoring.

FOLLOW-UP AFTER CLIENT CONTACT

Follow-up after client contact is follow-up after the second type of termination, that is, after the social worker has ceased working with the case. There are three related conditions under which follow-up can occur after a case has been terminated. In the first condition, follow-up is a planned part of the intervention process, a fading procedure with a single client. The intervention contacts are purposely spaced at longer intervals to determine whether the client can maintain the gains made during the intervention phase, but with reduced social work contact. If the client shows deterioration on dependent variables related to intervention objectives, intervention contacts are again made more frequently. In contrast, the maintenance of functioning would indicate that intervals between contacts might be spaced even longer or that there should be termination of follow-up. For example, intervention interviews may have been spaced one week apart for three months with a family. The objectives were achieved at the end of three months, and fading was instituted by having two more interventions, spaced one month apart. If the gains are maintained at these two follow-up points, a third follow-up might be scheduled six months later.

Closely related to the first condition is the condition of scheduled follow-up for a client unit (family, group, individual). This is planned at the completion of a fading procedure or at the termination of intervention, which may not have incorporated a fading procedure. The purpose of this follow-up is to obtain information regarding maintenance of client progress as well as data concerning new problems or difficulties the client might be experiencing. The third condition is one of follow-up, but one that was not planned with a client at termination of intervention. Typically, groups of clients are surveyed for the purpose of identifying maintenance of progress, new difficulties, problems related to service delivery, and gaps in service.

LOCATING AND CONTACTING CLIENTS

Clients who terminate services at a social agency often move or may even wish to discontinue having further contacts with social workers, particularly if there is dissatisfaction with the services that were provided. Social workers who wish to gather follow-up information need to plan how to best locate clients. For planned fading and scheduled follow-up (conditions 1 and 2), the social worker should involve the client in the planning for follow-up. At termination, the client should be told if there is to be follow-up. The rationale for follow-up (such as checking on client maintenance of gains, or providing an opportunity for the client to discuss her/his experience and future plans) should be provided, and the nature of the follow-up itself should be discussed. The client will want to know when and where the follow-up will occur, the types of data to be gathered, and the length of the interview. The worker and client should discuss a tentative date, noting that it can be changed, if necessary. They also should determine the most convenient place for the client to have a follow-up interview. Clients should be given self-stamped change of address postcards in the event they move, and should be told what the follow-up procedures would be. As an example of possible follow-up procedures, about a month prior to the follow-up date, a letter could be sent to the client explaining again the purpose of follow-up and the procedures to be followed; one to two weeks before the follow-up, a telephone call could be made to serve as a reminder.

The worker may consider conducting telephone interviews, as opposed to individual visits, to collect follow-up information. Telephone interviews are less expensive than visits to clients' homes. They are especially useful for short interviews when information gathered is focused on a few questions related to intervention objectives. If telephone interviews are to be used, a particularly helpful procedure is to send the questions to clients before the actual telephone interview so they can consider their answers more carefully (Dillman, 1978).

When a follow-up study is not scheduled with the client at termination, it may be more difficult to carry out the study. If the purpose of the follow-up is to see how individual clients have progressed, this should be explained in a letter to the client, noting that the agency will call to set an appointment date.

If the purpose of this follow-up is to gather information about clients' perceptions of agency services as well as about their own needs and problems, the social worker may want to devise a questionnaire or a structured interview schedule. Questionnaires could be mailed to clients, providing them with the rationale for the study, as well as assurances regarding the confidentiality of individual respondents and the use of information only in aggregate form (such as averaging across clients). Questionnaires are less expensive than telephone interviews, which in turn are less expensive than interviews in clients' homes. Response rates are higher, however, for personal interviews than for telephone interviews and questionnaires. Response rates should be more than 50%, preferably 75-80% if one wishes to argue that those who responded are representative of the group of clients who are included in the follow-up study. Response rates to questionnaires can be increased by mailing second and even third letters or postcards reminding respondents to respond to the survey. Dillman (1978) provides other suggestions for increasing response rates.

SAMPLING

A social worker seeking to follow-up a group of clients may not have the time or resources to interview all of them. This is especially the case when follow-up is not scheduled for clients and when the social worker is seeking answers to questions from many clients who received services from the agency.

A sample can provide an indication of average responses of the total number of available clients. A sample is a smaller group, drawn from the population (the total pool of available clients) in such a way that the sample is representative of the population. Although there are many different strategies for drawing these samples (see "Sampling" by J.R. Seaburg, 1985), *simple random sampling* and *systematic sampling* are most useful for caseloads in social agencies. Both procedures require that the population of available clients be listed. If, for example, a social worker wishes to select a sample from clients seen in the past year, the names and addresses of those clients would be collected from the files. Then, the clients would be listed in alphabetical order. Suppose for illustrative purposes there are 200 clients listed. The size of the sample should be 30 or more and at least 1/10 or more of the population (Seaburg, 1985, p. 146). In this example, the smallest sample size would be 30. Suppose further that the worker has time and resources to obtain a sample of 50. The next step is to assign a number to each name that is alphabetized. Since there are 200 clients, the numbers would range from 001, assigned to client A, to 200, assigned to client Z.

Following *simple random sampling* procedures, the worker should consult a random numbers table, such as the excerpt produced in Table 6.1 from Random Number Tables by W. J. Dixon and F. J. Massey, Jr. (1957, p. 366). A table of random numbers has digits arranged so that there is an equal probability for selecting each number. Having decided on the population, 200, and the sample size, 50, the social worker selects 50 numbers from the list of 001 to 200 by arbitrarily starting at one point in the table and reading three numbers (since the clients were assigned

Table 6.1 Table of Random Numbers

10	09	73
37	54	20
08	42	26
99	01	90
12	80	79
66	06	57
31	06	01
85	26	97
63	57	33
73	79	64
98	52	01
11	80	50
83	45	29
88	68	54
99	59	46

SOURCE: "Random Number Tables" by W. J. Dixon and F. J. Massey, Jr. (1957, p. 366).

three-digit numbers) from the top to the bottom, then moving to the next set of three columns or digits until the sample of 50 is selected. Starting at the upper left hand corner of Table 6.1, the first number is 100, the second number, 375, is more than 200, so it is omitted, the third number, 084, is included, as are 128 and 118. Hence, names connected with 100, 084, 128, and 118 are included in the sample, and the process is continued until 50 names are selected.

In *systematic sampling,* the worker would choose every fourth name, so that 1 out of 4 in the population is chosen. To determine the selection fraction the sample size is divided by the population size (50/200 = 1/4 in this example). For the list of 200, the worker could also begin by choosing a starting point from a table of random numbers (001-200). Referring to Table 6.1, starting at the upper left hand corner, 100 would be the starting point. This would be included in the sample along with 104, 108, and so on. After reaching 200, the worker would go to the beginning (001) and proceed until 096, when 50 cases would have been selected.

CONTACTING CLIENTS

Once clients are identified and plans are made to contact them, the social worker should be very sensitive to the clients' needs. Clients may not want others to know about their involvement in social work intervention. They may be anxious during follow-up contacts for a variety of reasons, including the fear that they will be judged as in need of more intervention when they do not want it. The social worker should assure clients that they have the right to refuse to participate in providing information (except where it might be mandatory by law, such as in child abuse and protective custody cases) or, if appropriate, in engaging in further interventions.

It is especially important to secure client cooperation when information is desired that has no direct benefit for the client. The social worker may be interested in improving services for all clients if improvements are necessary. In this case, the worker must appeal to the client's altruism in trying to make services better for other clients. Pointing out to clients that their responses do not affect their right to treatment and that they will not be identified individually are helpful in allaying potential fears.

The social worker or interviewer should be prompt for all appointments and should immediately attend to arranging new appointments upon cancellations or nonappearances. Continued respect in an atmosphere of genuine concern are important attitudes to convey, because they help to build trust and elicit client cooperation.

INFORMATION

As when collecting follow-up information during on-going client contact, basic kinds of data to gather after termination of client contact are those that relate to the attainment of intervention objectives and those that are pertinent to continued assessment and reassessment. Additional data that are often gathered pertain to clients' opinions about the services they received, as well as their evaluation of gaps in service and possible strengths and weaknesses in the services that were provided.

Existing instruments for assessing client satisfaction such as that developed by Larsen et al. (1979) might be employed, or workers might develop their own questionnaire and rating scales, using concepts and principles discussed in Chapters 3 and 4. Since the time for follow-up is limited and long, tiring questionnaires and interviews work against good response rates and thoughtful answers, it is important for workers to develop very specific sets of questions that are easy for clients to understand and are focused on specific concerns that clients might have. Questions can be asked about the ingredients that make for quality services, such as how much the services helped clients in their daily functioning at home, on the job, with friends, at school; the extent to which clients were satisfied with the services they received, to such an extent that they would refer friends and relations to the agency and return themselves if future problems develop; and opinions about the social worker(s) from whom they received interventions.

For questionnaires and personal contact interviews, simple 4 to 5-point rating scales can be used as responses to a series of questions about the agency. A rating scale could be adapted from a follow-up study routinely conducted in an Ypsilanti, Michigan restaurant. Following the meal (a food intervention), a card with questions on it about the food (services) and the waitress (service provider) is given to customers to register their opinions. The response system is illustrated in Figure 6.2. These faces are intended to range from very satisfied to very dissatisfied. A scale such as this is simple to understand and can be used for children as well as adults, when appropriate instructions are included.

Of course, satisfaction with services does not necessarily correlate with effectiveness of interventions (Larsen et al., 1979). Clients who confront difficult issues in their lives may experience great discomfort while receiving social work interventions; and that discomfort may, some conjecture, be necessary before clients can change (no pain, no gain!). Hence, it is important for the social worker to be aware that both satisfaction data and effectiveness data should be gathered and that satisfaction data should not be allowed to substitute for client effectiveness. It is progress with the client's problems that social workers should be mainly concerned about. On the other hand, satisfaction data can be useful when they are summarized for groups of clients. They can indicate whether there is a problem in service delivery, such as inconvenient client appointment times and lack of transportation. They can point to problems in communication and understanding between worker and client. They can provide clues as to why interventions are effective or not effective. They serve as a screen which detects potential problems, particularly if a large majority of clients are dissatisfied with the interventions they receive.

DATA ANALYSIS AND INFERENCES

Procedures for analyzing data for attainment of intervention objectives for single client units are the same as discussed earlier regarding follow-up during client contact. If, as often is the case, there are

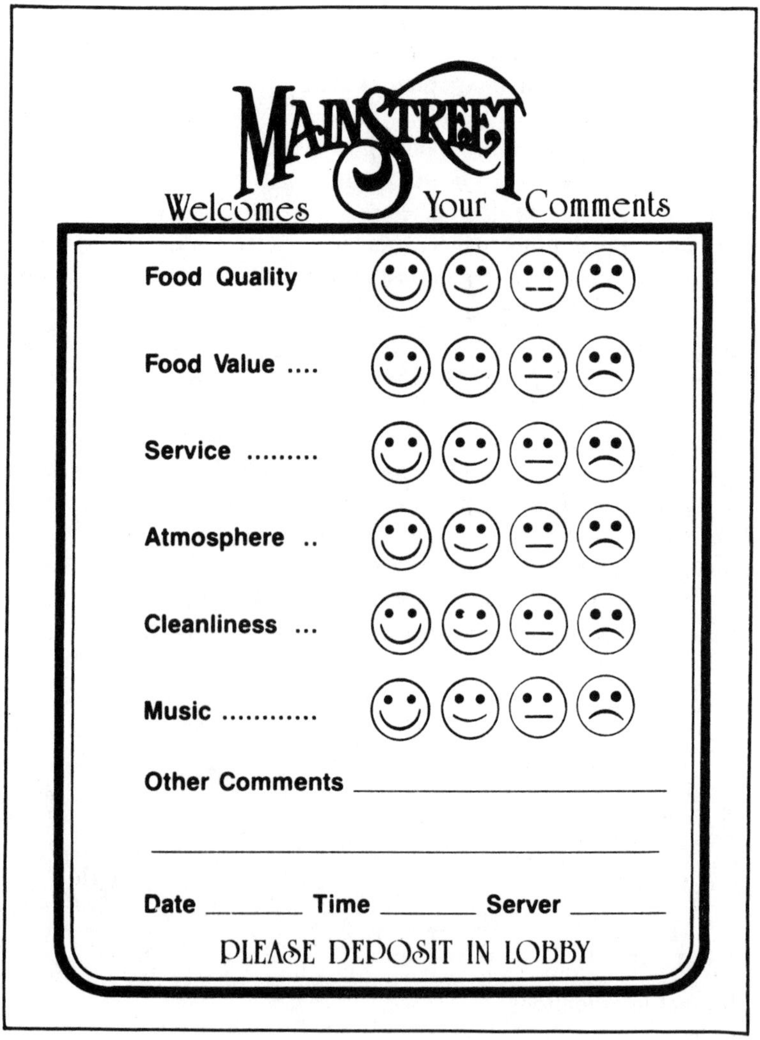
MAINSTREET Welcomes Your Comments

Food Quality

Food Value ....

Service ....

Atmosphere ..

Cleanliness ...

Music ....

Other Comments ______________________

____

Date ________ Time ________ Server ________

PLEASE DEPOSIT IN LOBBY

Figure 6.2

multiple sets of dependent variables about which data are gathered at follow-up, separate analyses are carried out for each dependent variable. Thus, it is possible for interventions to be differentially effective. When data are gathered to reflect on opinions or perceptions for a group of clients, then data should be analyzed by aggregating (combining) them. To illustrate, assume clients answer 10 questions about the degree to which they are satisfied with various ingredients of agency interventions (such as worker respect, promptness, agency office hours, frequency and length of each contact with the worker), and to explain their answers. Assume further that there are 50 clients responding to this survey. For each question, the worker can indicate the number and percentage of respondents who are satisfied. Twenty-five clients (50%) may have been neither satisfied not dissatisfied, 10 clients (20%) may have been satisfied, 10 clients (20%) very satisfied, and 5 clients (10%) dissatisfied. Percentages, proportions, means, and medians should be used to reflect central tendency and ranges of responses to indicate dispersion. The clients' explanations for their reported satisfaction/dissatisfaction can be analyzed by their thematic contents. The worker would read the responses, looking for themes and then count the number of clients making similar responses. For example, of 50 clients expressing neither satisfaction nor dissatisfaction, 25 might have indicated that they didn't receive enough intervention contact to make an adequate judgment of contact, 15 might not have responded, and the reasons given by 10 clients may not have been able to be grouped by a single category.

PRACTICE-RELATED AND PROGRAMMATIC DECISIONS

The major *practice-related* decisions that are affected by follow-up information are those involving the reinstatement of intervention and the provision of additional interventions based on modifications of the assessment. Interventions should be reinstated if there is deterioration, the client wants services and, in the worker's judgment, a reinstated intervention will continue to be effective. In addition to the original problem, new problems may be uncovered which lead to modified or additional interventions.

Perhaps the original problem is resolved and gains continue to be maintained in follow-up, but there are severe, new problems. In this instance, the worker must decide whether to be reinvolved with the client, or to refer the client to another worker or agency. Relevant information from follow-up would include the nature of the new problems, their severity and duration, as well as the willingness of the client to work on those problems with the social worker. If there is not enough information from follow-up, the social worker may decide to set up another interview for the specific purpose of further assessment to decide whether the worker's services are adequate for the particular client's needs.

Programmatic decisions are those involving changes in agency practices and policies that involve more than one worker and more than one client unit, and can grow out of follow-up data such as these. Relevant information may be obtained from either scheduled or nonscheduled follow-up interviews in which gaps in service are indicated, as well as aids and barriers to effective uses of services. Aggregated data describing client satisfaction or dissatisfaction with agency practices may lead to programmatic changes such as scheduling specific services at different times.

Follow-up information need not be negative. It may provide indications of well-received, effective interventions. If so, the information should be documented and distributed to other social workers in the same agency. Success stories should be compiled regarding the effectiveness of intervention with clients.

From time to time, data from single client units should be reviewed for purposes of discerning communalities with differences within and between interventions. In particular, one can explore and examine similarities and differences based on groupings that are significant for the worker and agency. For example, the worker and agency administration might be interested in the extent to which there are indications of differential success between workers of different ethnic status. Cases might then be compiled for workers and their clients of same and different ethnic statuses. Client satisfaction questionnaires might also be obtained for groups of different clients of those workers, and questionnaires regarding worker and client concerns about ethnic similarities and differences could be constructed. Aggregate data could be described and compared.

EXERCISES

1. For one of your clients, devise a plan to analyze progress in achieving intervention objectives, after intervention has been terminated.
2. Indicate how one can analyze data to make inferences about the maintenance of clinically significant and statistically significant changes during follow-up.

3. Select a sample of clients from a social agency by employing a systematic sampling procedure.

4. Specify several internal validity threats you would need to consider when trying to infer causality for a designated intervention and a specific client outcome.

5. Construct a questionnaire that you could use for assessing client satisfaction/dissatisfaction with social services.

REFERENCES

Aero, R., & Weiner, E. (1981). *The mind test.* New York: William Morrow.

Anastasi, A. (1976). *Psychological testing,* 2nd Ed. New York: Macmillan.

Barlow, D. H., & Hersen, M. (1984). *Single case experimental designs: Strategies for studying behavior change,* 2nd Ed. New York: Pergamon.

Berlin, S. B. (1978). *An investigation of the effects of cognitive-behavior modification treatments on problems of inappropriate self-criticism among women.* Unpublished doctoral dissertation, University of Washington.

Berlin, S. B. (1985). Maintaining reduced levels of self-criticism through relapse prevention treatment. *Social Work Research & Abstracts, 21*(1), 21-33.

Billingsley, F., White, O. R., & Munson, R. (1980). Procedural reliability: A rationale and an example. *Behavioral Assessment, 2,* 229-241.

Bloom, M., & Fischer, J. (1982). *Evaluating practice: Guidelines for the accountable professional.* Englewood Cliffs, NJ: Prentice-Hall.

Bostwick, G. J., Jr., & Kyte, N. S. (1985). Measurement. In Grinnel, R. M., Jr. (Ed.), *Social work research and evaluation,* 2nd Ed. (pp. 149-160). Itasca, IL: F. E. Peacock.

Briar, S. (1973). Effective social work intervention in direct practice: Implications for education. In *Facing the challenge: Plenary session papers from the 19th Annual Program Meeting.* New York: Council on Social Work Education.

Briar, S., & Miller, H. (1971). *Problems and issues in social casework.* New York: Columbia University Press.

Buros, O. K. (Ed.). (1978). *The eighth mental measurements yearbook.* Vols. I and II. Highland Park, NJ: Graphon Press.

Bronson, D. E., & Blythe, B. J. (1987). Computer support for single-case evaluation of practice. *Social Work Research & Abstracts, 23*(3), 10-13.

Campbell, D. T., & Stanley, J. C. (1963). *Experimental and quasi-experimental designs for research.* Chicago: Rand McNally.

Cook, T. D., & Campbell, D. T. (1979). *Quasi-experimentation: Design and analysis issues for field settings.* Chicago: Rand McNally.

Corcoran, K., & Fischer, J. (1987). *Measures for clinical practice: A sourcebook.* New York: The Free Press.

Davis, L. V. (1985). Female and male voices in social work. *Social Work, 30,* 106-113.

Diagnostic and statistical manual of mental disorders, 3rd Ed. (1980). Washington, DC: American Psychiatric Association.

Dillman, D. A. (1978). *Mail and telephone surveys.* New York: John Wiley.

Dixon, W. J., & Massey, F. J., Jr. (1957). *Introduction to statistical analysis,* 2nd Ed. New York: McGraw-Hill.

Ezell, M., & McNeece, C. A. (1986). Practice effectiveness: Research or rhetoric? *Social Work, 31,* 401-402.

Filstead, W. J. (Ed.). (1978). *Qualitative methodology.* Chicago: Markham.

Gambrill, E. D., Thomas, E. J., & Carter, R. D. (1971). Procedures for sociobehavioral practice in open settings. *Social Work, 16,* 51-62.

Gingerich, W. J. (1984). Generalizing single-case evaluation from classroom to practice. *Journal of Education for Social Work, 20*(1), 74-82.

Gingerich, W., & Feyerherm, W. (1979). The celeration line technique for assessing client change. *Journal of Social Service Research, 3,* 99-113.

Goldstein, H. K. (1962). Making practice more scientific through knowledge of research. *Social Work, 7,* 108-112.

Goldstein, H. K. (1963). *Research standards and methods for social workers.* New Orleans, LA: Hauser Press.

Gottman, J. M., & Leiblum, S. R. (1974). *How to do psychotherapy and how to evaluate it.* NY: Holt, Rinehart, and Winston.

Grinnell, R. M., Jr. (Ed.). (1985). *Social work research and evaluation,* 2nd Ed. Itasca, IL: F. E. Peacock.

Hartman, A. (1982). *Post-adoptive services to children and families.* Paper presented at the NASW Clinical Practice Conference, Washington, DC.

Hays, W. L. (1973). *Statistics for the social sciences,* 2nd Ed. New York: Holt, Rinehart and Winston.

Heineman, M. B. (1981). The obsolete scientific imperative in social work research. *Social Service Review, 55,* 371-397.

Hudson, W. W. (1982). *The clinical measurement package: A field manual.* Homewood, IL: Dorsey Press.

Hudson, W. W. (1985). Indexes and scales. In R. M. Grinnell, Jr. (Ed.), *Social work research and evaluation,* 2nd Ed. (pp. 185-205). Itasca, IL: F. E. Peacock.

Ivanoff, A., Blythe, B. J., & Briar, S. (1987). The empirical clinical practice debate. *Social Casework, 68,* 290-298.

Jacobson, N. S., Follette, W. C., & Revenstorf, D. (1984). Psychotherapy outcome research: Methods for reporting variability and evaluating clinical significance. *Behavior Therapy, 15,* 336-352.

Jayaratne, S. (1978) Analytic procedures for single-subject designs. *Social Work Research & Abstracts, 14*(3), 30-40.

Jayaratne, S., & Levy, R. L. (1979). *Empirical clinical practice.* New York: Columbia University Press.

Jayaratne, S., Tripodi, T., & Talsma, E. (1988). Comparative analysis and aggregation of single-case data. *Journal of Applied Behavioral Science, 24,* 119-128.

Kagle, J. D. (1982). Using single-subject measures in practice decisions: Systematic documentation or distortion? *Arete, 7,* 1-9.

Larsen, D. L., Attkisson, W. A., Hargreaves, W. A., & Nguyen, T. D. (1979). Assessment of client/patient satisfaction: Development of a general scale. *Evaluation and Program Planning, 2,* 197-207.

LeCroy, C. W., & Rose, S. D. (1986). Evaluation of preventive interventions for enhancing social competence in adolescents. *Social Work Research & Abstracts, 22*(2), 8-16.

Maas, H. S. (1979). Assessing family and child welfare practice. *Social Work, 24,* 365-372.

Magura, S., & Moses, B. S. (1986). *Outcome measures for child welfare services: Theory and applications.* Washington, DC: Child Welfare League of America.

McMahon, P. M. (1987). Shifts in intervention procedures: A problem in evaluating human service interventions. *Social Work Research & Abstracts, 23*(4), 13-16.

Meyer, C. H. (1984). Integrating research and practice. (Editorial Page). *Social Work, 29,* 323.

Nelsen, J. C. (1983). *Family treatment: An integrative approach.* Englewood Cliffs, NJ: Prentice-Hall.

Parsonson, B., & Baer, D. (1978). The analysis and presentation of graphic data. In T. R. Kratochwill (Ed.), *Single subject research* (pp. 101-161). NY: Academic Press.

Peterson, L., Homer, A. L., & Wonderlich, S. A. (1982). The integrity of independent variables in behavior analysis. *Journal of Applied Behavior Analysis, 15,* 477-492.

Piers, E. V. (1984). *Piers-Harris Children's Self-Concept Scale.* Los Angeles: Western Psychological Services.

Richey, C. A., Blythe, B. J., & Berlin, S. B. (1987). Do social workers evaluate their practice? *Social Work Research & Abstracts, 23*(2), 14-20.

Robins, L. N., & Helzer, J. E. (1986). Diagnosis and clinical assessment: The current state of psychiatric diagnosis. *Annual Review of Psychology, 37,* 409-432.

Rubin, A. (1986). Tunnel vision in the search for effective interventions: Rubin responds. *Social Work, 31,* 403-404.

Ruckdeschel, R. A., & Farris, B. E. (1981). Assessing practice: A critical look at the single-case design. *Social Casework, 62,* 413-419.

Salend, S. J. (1984). Therapy outcome research: Threats to treatment integrity. *Behavior Modification, 8,* 211-222.

Seaburg, J. R. (1985). Sampling. In R. M. Grinnell, Jr. (Ed.), *Social work research and evaluation,* 2nd Ed. (pp. 133-148). Itasca, IL: F. E. Peacock.

Siegel, D. H. (1984). Defining empirically based practice. *Social Work, 29,* 325-331.

Siegel, S. (1956). *Nonparametric statistics for the behavioral sciences.* NY: McGraw-Hill.

Spielberger, C. D., Gorsuch, R. L., & Lushene, R. (1970). *STAI Manual.* Palo Alto, CA: Consulting Psychologists.

Thomas, E. J. (1977). The BESDAS Model for effective practice. *Social Work Research & Abstracts, 13*(2), 12-16.

Thomas, E. J. (1978). Research and service in single-case experimentation: Conflicts and choices. *Social Work Research & Abstracts, 14*(4), 20-31.

Thomas, E. J. (1984). *Designing interventions for the helping professions.* Beverly Hills, CA: Sage.

Thomas, E. J., Bastien, J., Stuebe, D. R., Bronson, D. E., & Yaffe, J. (1987). Assessing procedural descriptiveness: Rationale and illustrative study. *Behavioral Assessment, 9,* 43-56.

Tripodi, T. (1974). *Uses and abuses of social research in social work.* New York: Columbia University Press.

Tripodi, T. (1983). *Evaluative research for social workers.* Englewood Cliffs, NJ: Prentice-Hall.

Tripodi, T. (1988). *A typology of research knowledge for relating research to social work practice.* Paper presented at the 90th Anniversary of the Columbia University School of Social Work, New York.

Tripodi, T., & Epstein, I. (1978). Incorporating knowledge of research methodology into social work practice. *Journal of Social Service Research, 2,* 65-78.

Tripodi, T., & Epstein, I. (1980). *Research techniques for clinical social workers.* New York: Columbia University Press.

Upper, D. J., & Cautela, J. R. (1975). The process of individual behavior therapy. In
    M. Hersen, R. M. Eisler, & P. M. Miller (Eds.), *Progress in behavior modification*,
    Vol. I. New York: Academic Press.
Walker, H., & Lev, J. (1953). *Statistical inference*. NY: Holt, Rinehart, and Winston.
Wedenoja, M., Nurius, P. S., & Tripodi, T. (1988). Enhancing mindfulness in practice
    prescriptive thinking. *Social Casework, 69,* 427-433.

ABOUT THE AUTHORS

Betty J. Blythe, M.S.W., A.C.S.W., Ph.D., is Associate Professor at the University of Pittsburgh School of Social Work, where she teaches interpersonal practice methods and clinical research. She has conducted empirically based practice and intervention research in a variety of social agencies and has published numerous articles and chapters concerned with the design and testing of social work interventions. A member of a recent national committee that integrated content from home-based services for high risk families into social work education, Dr. Blythe is currently on the editorial board of the *Journal of Social Work Education* and provides editorial consultation to several professional publications.

Tony Tripodi, M.S.W., A.C.S.W., D.S.W., is Associate Dean of Academic Affairs and Professor of Social Work, also at the University of Pittsburgh. He has conducted research on clinical judgment, psychotherapy, program evaluation, research methodology, and the utilization of research methods by social workers. Dr. Tripodi served as a research and evaluation consultant for national and international organizations, including the European Common Market and the Zancan Foundation in Padova, Italy, and he is currently a member of the Task Force on Social Work Research, National Institute of Mental Health, and the National Research Advisory Committee, Boysville, Michigan. Previously editor-in-chief of *Social Work Research and Abstracts,* he serves on the book committee of the National Association of Social Workers and on the editorial boards of several professional journals. He has a wide range of experience in teaching social work research courses and has published extensively.